MENTAL HEALTH

BIOLOGY

AGENCY

MEANING

THERAN PRESS

Theran Press is the academic publishing imprint of Silver Goat Media.

Theran is dedicated to authentic partnerships with our academic associates, to the quality design of scholarly books, and to elite standards of peer review.

Theran Seeks to free intellectuals from the confines of traditional publishing.

Theran scholars are authorities and revolutionaries in their respective fields.

Theran encourages new models for generating and distributing knowledge.

For our creatives, for our communities, for our world.

WWW.THERANPRESS.ORG

This book was designed and produced by Silver Goat Media, LLC. Fargo, ND U.S.A. www.silvergoatmedia.com. SGM, the SGM goat, Theran Press, and the Theran theta are trademarks of Silver Goat Media, LLC.

Cover design: Travis Klath © 2019 SGM.
Book interior design and typesetting in Palatino Linotype by Cady Ann Rutter.

ISBN-10: 1-944296-12-3 ISBN-13: 978-1-944296-12-4

A portion of the annual proceeds from the sale of this book is donated to the Longspur Prairie Fund. www.longspurprairie.org

Printed and bound in the United States of America.

MENTAL HEALTH

BIOLOGY, AGENCY, MEANING

William Schultz

THERAN PRESS

For my family.

Table of Contents

☀ Acknowledgments

I wouldn't have completed this book without the encouragement and help of my brother, Peter. My family has always supported me, especially my parents. Elizabeth Parker enriches and motivates me every day. Jean Eich has provided insight, wisdom, and a model of clinical skill. Richard Gilmore taught me important lessons about thinking and writing. Rhodz encouraged me during moments of defeat. Irving Kirsch and Brett Deacon inspired my research. Jesse Haksgaard is a pillar of strength; Fernando B. de Moura is a model of perseverance. Sandie Wick has offered great support. For the past six years, Mark Carlson-Ghost, Jim Theisen, Jeffrey Brown, and Rajkumari David have nurtured and mentored me. Nicholas Griffith, BraVada Garrett-Akinsanya, and Pearl Barner II guided me. David Kelley encouraged and supported my research.

The chapters in this book are heavily revised versions of work published in previous forms; these are listed in the bibliography as: Schultz (2015, August); Schultz (2015)a; Schultz (2015)b; Schultz (2016); Schultz & Hunter (2016)a; Schultz and Hunter (2016)b; Schultz 2017; and Schultz 2018. For permission to reproduce, the author is grateful to the editors and editorial boards of *Mad in America*, the *Journal of Humanistic Psychology*, *Ethical Human Psychology and Psychiatry*, the *Journal of Feminist Family Therapy*, *Reason Papers*, and *The Behavior Therapist*.

☀ Introduction

The past twenty years have manifested worrying trends in the field of mental health in the United States. Most concerning is the increasingly popular idea that mental disorders are best understood as brain disorders. From this point of view, when confronted with an overly-energetic little boy, parents are informed that their son has a "brain disease" which causes inattention and hyperactivity and that this disease is best treated with drugs. Likewise, a person suffering from a major depressive disorder is told that her depression is caused by a "chemical imbalance" in her brain and that this imbalance is best treated with other chemicals that can restore equilibrium to her brain's chemistry. In a similar fashion, a young man afflicted with severe obsessive-compulsive disorder is advised that his brain is "malfunctioning" and that this malfunction is best corrected by a pill. Most of us have heard stories like these, either from our own doctors or from people we love. The idea is not just common—it is ubiquitous. "Everyone knows that mental illness is caused by the brain; those are the facts."

And therein lies the problem.

Those are *not* the facts.

The notion that mental disorders are best understood as brain disorders is *not* supported by the empirical evidence. Indeed, the opposite is true. Both philosophical argument and the scientific data strongly suggest that mental disorders are best understood *not* as brain disorders, but rather as solvable problems of personal agency and meaning.

This book shows some of the reasons why this is true and, more importantly, why this truth matters.

This project began during my own studies in the field of mental health, a professional area that I've engaged as a patient, as a researcher, and as a clinician. As a patient, my experience with obsessive-compulsive disorder devastated me. As I looked for help, I was repeatedly told that I had a chemical imbalance in my brain. This chemical imbalance necessitated medication, I was told, medication that I'd potentially be taking for the rest of my life. But what evidence supported this assertion? Was there any truth to this story? How would I know the truth when—and if—I found it? My own quest for answers to these questions became the first steps of my journey towards becoming a scholar of mental health and a practicing clinician.

One of the most important stops on my journey was arriving at a *theory of mental disorder*.

When those of us in the mental health field conduct our work, when we're trying to help our clients, or when we're trying to figure out what might be wrong with our patients, we rely upon various theories regarding the causes of mental disorders. These theories provide a road map that we use to guide our efforts to assist our patients' healing. Two dominant theories regarding the nature of mental disorders are illustrated below:

> A psychiatrist working at a hospital emergency room encounters a 30-year-old woman, brought in by her family, clearly experiencing emotional distress. She's disorientated, she's experiencing grandiose delusions, and—according to her family members' reports—she's undergone a significant emotional and behavioral transformation; she's not the same person. The psychiatrist suspects a psychotic disorder. However, other symptoms are present: urinary incontinence, vision problems, and muscle spasms. A thorough set of blood tests are conducted. These tests reveal that the patient has neurosyphilis. A bacterial infection has reached her brain and is causing her disorientation, her delusions, and her behavioral changes. Upon the administration of antibiotics, the symptoms disappear—although some permanent effects may remain because of physical brain damage.

Clearly, some mental disorders are best explained by pathology in the brain. In the case above, the patient had neurosyphilis; antibiotics were the cure.

When it comes to clinical practice, some mental health professionals believe that this kind of story can be useful not only for treating a disease, like neurosyphilis, but also for treating other mental disorders, like schizophrenia, major depressive disorder, or generalized anxiety disorder. Again, as noted, the idea that "mental disorders are brain disorders" has become an increasingly influential theoretical model for explaining and treating mental illness. Perhaps the best evidence of this is the recent emergence of the National Institute of Mental Health's new research program, the Research Domain Criteria Project (RDoC), which specifically conceptualizes mental disorders as disordered brain circuits.

There's much to gain from this theoretical stance and in certain cases, like the story told above, this approach is the only one that works. Yet consider a second story:

> A psychiatrist is sought in consultation by an older man who's experiencing a collection of depressive symptoms: sadness, lack of energy, loss of interest in activities previously enjoyed, difficulty sleeping, appetite change, difficulty concentrating, and guilt. The psychiatrist elicits further information and discovers that the man's wife, whom he loved beyond words, died some time ago. Since that time, his sadness has grown; it has worn him down. He's not sure how much longer he can bear it.
>
> Eventually, the psychiatrist asks the man how his wife might have felt if he had been the one who died first. The man thinks for a moment, then replies that he believes she would have suffered enormously, just as he is now.
>
> The psychiatrist then wonders aloud:
>
> "Could it be that by being the one left alive, by being the one left to bear your suffering, that you're sparing your wife this painful experience?"
>
> Upon hearing this, the man's demeanor promptly and powerfully changes. He stands up, shakes the psychiatrist's hand, and leaves the office.[1]

This story suggests that the man's suffering was best understood *not* as disordered brain circuits—as broken biology—but rather as a crisis of agency and meaning induced by emotional pain—pain seemingly without purpose. This interpretation was confirmed by the case study. Once the man's pain had a purpose, he found both agency and meaning in his experience; he was remoralized.

Both stories present cases of emotional distress. More importantly, both stories illustrate the way that mental disorders are theorized and how these theories guide treatment.

But how do we know which theory is the "right" one? How do we pick? Should we pick at all?

Here, it's important to understand that most mental disorders do not have a causal explanation as straightforward as neurosyphilis. In fact, the Bible of mental health—the American Psychiatric Association's *Diagnostic and Statistical Manual of Mental Disorders – Fifth Edition* is agnostic regarding the causal story of almost all mental disorders. This state of understanding has led many mental health professionals to adopt the view that mental disorders are caused by a combination of biological, environmental, and psychological components. This way of thinking about mental disorders—*the biopsychosocial model*—is now predominate. Yet, with the ascendancy of biological conceptualizations of mental health, the biopsychosocial model has been increasingly criticized as being uninformative and as contributing to a dangerous eclecticism which can hinder appropriate healing. If this is true, then disentangling the ways in which the biological, psychological, and social components contribute to a patient's mental health is of critical importance.

The chapters of this book explore the way these components contribute to the manifestation of mental disorders and their treatment.

In the first chapter, "Child-Centered Play Therapy," I examine emotional and behavioral disturbance in children. Here, I detail the theory and practice of child-centered play therapy (CCPT). CCPT suggests that play, combined with a therapeutic relationship based on unconditional acceptance, is a principal component of improving the lives of children with emotional and behavioral difficulties. This approach has been used with children experiencing a span of presenting concerns, from ADHD to conduct disorders. I describe the outcome studies which substantiate the theoretical basis of CCPT and connect this to my criticism of approaches which favor medication. There are alternatives to sometimes dangerous medications used to address children's emotional and behavioral challenges. Most importantly, providing children a space where they can be themselves, and be seen and accepted while they are themselves, has incredible healing power.

In Chapter Two, "Mental Disorders and Genetics," I focus on genetic explanations of mental disorders by way of a specific example: the genetic explanation of binge eating. A genetic explanation of binge-eating looks like this: While those who experience binge-eating are often blamed by others and themselves as lacking self-control or will-power, evidence suggests that binge eating is significantly influenced by genetic predisposition. If this is true, then much of the blaming associated with lack of self-control is inaccurate, probably harmful, and should be stopped. This chapter explores the way in which genetic contributions to mental disorders are established and provides commentary on this process and some of its implications. Genetic etiologies of mental disorders are still in their infancy. Over emphasizing genetic etiologies is both inaccurate and dangerous. Etiologies which emphasize agency and meaning contribute to increased self-efficacy and positive treatment outcomes.

"Mental Disorders and Brain Scan Research" is the subject of Chapter Three. Here, a review of the current state of brain-based research on mental disorders is conducted. Brain imaging technology has contributed to an explosion of research related to mental disorders. This research focuses on how the brains of those diagnosed with mental disorders are different than healthy individuals. By identifying brain differences, it is hoped we can better understand causes and cures. However, my co-author, Noel Hunter, and I suggest there are important reasons for caution and concern. Neuroscience has not identified any clinically actionable brain differences for mental disorders. If, in the future, brain differences are reliably found, neuroscientists will need to develop methods to disentangle confounders related to top-down causation. Until then, emphasizing brain differences involved in mental disorders is premature and dangerous.

In Chapter Four, "Depression and the Chemical Imbalance Hypothesis," I describe a common explanation of depression: that it's caused by an imbalance of neurotransmitters in the brain. What causes depression? According to the chemical imbalance hypothesis, it's not enough serotonin, dopamine, norepinephrine, and/or other neurotransmitters in the brain. What can we do to help? Raise the level of their neurotransmitters—usually via antidepressant medication. The evidence for the chemical imbalance hypothesis is weak and the large majority of Americans who believe that a chemical imbalance causes depression are misinformed. This chapter takes a step to correct that misinformation.

Noel Hunter and I integrate research on the chemical imbalance hypothesis to feminist interpretations of depression in Chapter Five, "Depression and Feminism." Broadly understood, many feminists view depression primarily as a manifestation of social problems, not individual shortcomings, such as malfunctioning brains. From this perspective, it's seen as convenient for those entrenched in current hierarchies to instruct women—who are diagnosed with depression at far higher rates than men: "It's not a problem with our social structure, it's that your brain is broken." It may be true that one day we are able to identify malfunctioning brains which directly cause depression. Until then, asserting that many, most, or all women's depression is caused by their brains is not supported by the evidence, can have negative clinical impacts, and risks increased marginalization of social contributors to distress.

Chapter Six, "Explaining Depression in Clinical Settings," treats the prevalence of two explanatory analogies of depression in medical settings. Unfortunately, the evidence I review suggests that misleading and potentially dangerous explanations for depression are commonly provided. Medical doctors, especially general practitioners, are the largest prescribers of antidepressants. They also are often not well-read regarding the mental health literature (think of all the other health related areas of which they are expected to be knowledgeable). This chapter provides valuable information to doctors and their patients.

In Chapter Seven, "Mental Disorders and Stigma," I explore the relationship between explaining mental disorders as biologically caused phenomena and mental health stigma. Mental disorders are highly stigmatized. For those experiencing mental disorders, stigma increases distress and discourages help-seeking behavior. Reducing stigma is valuable. One popular approach attempting to reduce stigma is to focus on the biological causes of mental disorders, with the hope that this will reduce the frequency those suffering from such disorders encounter claims that they are somehow at fault (e.g. weak-willed, too sensitive, just need to snap out of it) for their condition. Unfortunately, the story is significantly more complicated. Emphasizing biogenetic etiologies of mental disorders can have positive effects on self-blame but it does not decrease stigma and advocates of this approach to reducing stigma may be doing more harm than good.

"Neuroessentialism: Theoretical and Clinical Considerations," is the topic of Chapter Eight. Here, I review recent and significant changes in federally funded mental disorder research. These changes leave behind previous approaches to mental disorders, which focus on presenting symptoms, and instead focus on an etiology of mental disorders which assumes that mental disorders are biological conditions: fundamentally, disordered brain circuits. This approach has multiple motivations, implications, and clinical consequences which I review in turn.

Finally, in Chapter Nine, I discuss implications of the preceding chapters. Not only do biogenetic etiologies rely on questionable philosophic assumptions and weak scientific data, they're also associated with increased prognostic pessimism. In other words, the more someone believes their mental disorder is biogenetically caused, the less likely they are to expect improvement. This is important. Someone's expectancy for the future is an important contributor to their actual future; the data shows this to be true. Those who *expect* to do better, *do* better.

In addition to my concerns regarding prognostic pessimism, I also fear that by writing off experiences of distress as brain disorders, we rob those experiencing distress of identifying meaningful components of their distress and meaningful ways their agency can transcend that distress. From this point of view, important human virtues—such as empathy, courage, and fortitude—can be cultivated within the chaos and pain of distress, allowing a more robust and comprehensive self to blossom.

Chapter One
Child-Centered Play Therapy

"Henry" is a nine-year-old Hispanic boy from a low-income family.[2] He presented with numerous emotional and behavioral problems at home and school. He was commonly disobedient. He frequently threw tantrums. He often became aggressive with peers. He occasionally stole from family, teachers, and classmates. An intake interview with Henry's guardian revealed that he was a middle child of four siblings. Henry's mother was in jail, and his father did not live with his family and had little contact. The family had a long record of interactions with the police.

When I first met Henry, he refused to talk to me until I performed push-ups in front of him. After that, he agreed to play games with me, such as Jenga and checkers. After a month of playing games, Henry's play interests changed to pretend cooking, and he used the play kitchen set to cook a variety of meals. A few weeks later, Henry invited me to cook with him. He told me I needed to cook well so that we could feed all the customers and keep them happy. He told me that if a customer became upset with me, he would keep me safe. After several weeks of primarily cooking-focused play, Henry transitioned to playing in the sand tray—a 3x3 foot table with a 6-inch deep sand pit. In the sand tray, play often focused on a family of toy turtles and their interactions with a variety of other animals. Typical themes of play included the baby turtle seeing things the mother and father turtle could not (and the disputes that arose because of this incongruity); the mother and father turtle being abducted—for one reason or another—from the pit; and other animals befriending, attacking, feeding, or playing with the turtle family. Henry often identified with a small plastic bird that had the power to turn invisible and fly over the sand and that commented on the interactions of the turtle family and their environment. During this six-month relationship, Henry's teachers and school staff reported that his emotional dysregulation and problematic behavior had been dramatically reduced.

I was practicing Child-Centered Play Therapy (CCPT) with Henry. Like most psychotherapies, CCPT posits underlying psychotherapeutic mechanisms thought to cause emotional, cognitive, and behavioral changes. In contrast to more directive psychotherapies, such as cognitive-behavioral therapy (CBT), which emphasize belief modification, behavior modification, and skill-building as crucial mechanisms,[3] CCPT posits that *play*—within a secure environment and in the presence of an accepting therapist—is the primary mechanism of change. An examination of the concepts "play," "secure environment," and "accepting therapist" will illuminate these mechanisms.

Play is a deceptively simple concept, difficult to define.[4] One reason is that it seems to include a wide variety of behaviors. For instance, sensorimotor play is characterized by repeated interactions with an object(s), such as a child putting a star-shaped block into a star-shaped slot.[5] Rough-and-tumble play includes behavior such as climbing, chasing, and play fighting.[6] Fantasy and pretend typically unfold in narrative sequences and often involve props, such as dolls, miniatures, or a toy stove.[7]

Many attempts have been made to refine and integrate the concept of play. One approach is to integrate behavior with consequences. For example, sometimes play fighting and real fighting are difficult to distinguish. However, if two children remain together and friendly after the conclusion of a "fight," then it is best characterized as play rather than aggression.[8] Another influential observation is that play behavior does not appear to serve an immediate purpose. From this perspective, non-instrumentality—doing something for its own sake—is a central characteristic of play.[9]

Even if we assume that non-instrumentality is a necessary feature of play, it is also true that children benefit from it in many ways. For instance, play encourages self-regulation of attention, emotion, and behavior.[10] It provides children a time during which they, not their parents, teachers, or instructional materials, guide experience and decision-making. This type of experience encourages the development of metacognitive and self-regulatory skills, which, in turn, support the growth of other skills such as problem-solving.[11] Self-regulated experience can also be important in educational development. For example, literacy education necessarily includes structured instruction in letter recognition, decoding, and reading.

Yet, it is also important to give children space and time to experiment with their newly developing literacy skills outside of structured instruction. This setting allows children to broaden and deepen their understanding in a way that is more effective than "top-down didactic transmission."[12] The beneficial effects of play have been documented in math,[13] geometric knowledge,[14] and general academic achievement,[15] as well as in emotional competence[16] and social competence.[17]

In the context of CCPT, the central feature of play is that it is an intrinsically motivated activity that is intrinsically complete:[18] To the greatest extent possible, the therapist allows the child to dictate the course of each therapy session, such as choosing the type of play to participate in and following along within that form of play. In the Henry's example, play includes activities ranging from participating in board games to pretend cooking to activities in the sand tray. All the while I attended him and followed his direction.

A secure environment is a physically safe space of the play-therapy room. A child in CCPT should be able predict and understand what unfolds within a play-therapy room. It is hoped that the child quickly learns that he is in control of the play-therapy room—that this is his space to *be*.

Intimately related to a secure environment is the presence of an accepting therapist.[19] Virginia Axline, a pioneer of CCPT, describes an accepting therapist's approach to working with a child as follows:

> In the play-therapy room, "no one criticizes what he does, no one nags, or suggests, or goads. . . . He can say anything that he feels like saying—and he is accepted completely. He can play with the toys in any way that he likes to—and he is accepted completely. He can hate and he can love and he can be as indifferent as the Great Stone Face—and he is still accepted completely.[20]

This radically accepting attitude is likely an unusual experience for a troubled child. In most circumstances, such as when the child is at home or at school, the child experiences a variety of demands. These demands can range from simple and probably unavoidable demands—such as eating, sleeping, and complying with commands—

to complicated processes such as navigating the emotional demands placed upon him by his guardians, siblings, friends, and teachers.[21] Consider, for example, the emotional demands faced by a child raised by an abusive father. Imagine the awareness a child likely develops in this context: noticing the triggers and cues that tend to precede abusive situations and developing an awareness of behavioral strategies to placate the father or avoid confrontation. Regardless of the demands on a specific child, due to the formative stage of children, demands are especially powerful experiences which are related to long-term neural, emotional, behavioral, and social development.[22]

Enter the accepting play therapist. The therapist does not bring the child more demands. The therapist does not demand that the child learn emotion-regulation techniques or cognitive-reframing strategies. The therapist does not demand that the child immediately or quickly adopt new feelings or new behaviors. The therapist holds a space for the child to manifest his own identity separate from the problems the child typically experiences and then bears witness to that manifestation.[23] Underlying this approach is the belief that the child "has within himself . . . the ability to solve his own problems."[24] As a result, the therapist "grants the individual the permissiveness to be himself; it accepts that self completely, without evaluation or pressure to change."[25]

From this perspective, a therapist's essential functions in therapy are to pay attention to the client, unconditionally accept the client,[26] communicate that attention and acceptance to the client (that is, demonstrate attention by stating factual descriptions of the child's behavior; for example, "You are paying close attention to what you're cooking in your frypan."), and demonstrate acceptance by adopting a non-judgmental attitude (that is, non-judgmentally commenting; for example, "The dinosaur killed the baby elephant even though the elephant asked it not to."). This non-directive approach nurtures a secure and warm relationship with the client.[27]

Underneath this non-directive assumption that a client can solve his own problems is belief in a developmental trajectory inherent within human beings which will unfold predictably unless obstructed.[28] This trajectory includes physical, cognitive, emotional, social, and play development. For instance, if a child's emotional development is obstructed because of a traumatic event or a chronically abusive relationship, the assumption underlying CCPT is that a child's inherent developmental drives can overcome the obstruction as long he is given the time and space to do so.

The inclusion of play development is instructive because it points to a central tenet of play therapy: Children process their inner experience through play.[29] Thus, as a child's inner experience deepens and matures, so does his play. For example, researchers have identified the relationship between the typical developmental milestones and diverse types of play activities. For instance, while manipulation of the physical environment is a predominant form of play for very young children, pretend play becomes dominant in children ages two - six. By age five, children's play typically includes multi-faceted fantasy which incorporates a variety of toys or other props.

Researchers have also identified familiar patterns in the progression of play within play therapy.[30] The case study of Henry is a good example of this progression. As therapy progressed and our relationship deepened, Henry's play transformed. At first, Henry was reluctant to speak with me, and we mostly played games. As our relationship grew, Henry transitioned from board games to pretend cooking to incorporating me into his pretend cooking within a narrative to the sand tray, in which in-depth interactions, usually involving families, were played out. This process highlights the development of the therapeutic relationship and the child processing his experiences. As Henry's trust in me grew, so did his emotional openness, evidenced by his incorporating me into his stories and involving me in the family dynamics of the miniatures in the sand tray. This transition within the play-therapy room was accompanied by a significant reduction of Henry's problematic behavior at home and school.

Why Does Play Work in Therapy?

The case example of Henry is not unique; examples abound. And yet researchers are not sure why play contributes to positive treatment outcomes.[31] Play is almost certainly effective for a variety of reasons that are common to all forms of therapy, such as the therapeutic alliance and consistent and compassionate attention to the child.[32]

There are three prominent theories about why play specifically is a beneficial therapeutic intervention.[33]

First, there is a large body of research which strongly suggests a relationship between self-expression and well-being.[34] This research typically links self-expression to personal autonomy and self-determination, which both contribute to well-being.[35] Thus, therapeutic interventions which foster conditions for self-expression, such as a trusting and caring therapeutic relationship, could be expected to improve well-being. This is, in fact, what a wide variety of psychotherapy research has identified.[36] Understandably, child and adult self-expression in psychotherapy differs. Unlike many adults, children generally "do not have the vocabulary to accurately express their emotions or their understanding of situations."[37] As a result, children use play to communicate: "Toys are their words, and play is their language."[38] Thus, some of CCPT's psychotherapeutic effectiveness is likely related to creating an environment in which children can express themselves in a developmentally appropriate way.

Another possible mechanism contributing to the effectiveness of play is its role in developing self-regulation. Self-regulation encompasses an individual's ability to control and moderate pleasant and unpleasant emotions, and it contributes to an individual's sense of self.[39] Self-regulation is strongly associated with feelings of subjective well-being as well as better health and goal achievement.[40] Self-regulation includes processes such as response inhibition, cognitive flexibility, self-monitoring, and shifting focus.[41] Crucially, children develop response inhibition, cognitive flexibility, and other key skills via play.[42] For instance, toddlers often grab, manipulate, take apart, and reassemble objects or toys. This process is rudimentary cognitive flexibility. As children grow older and their play moves beyond simple object manipulation to imaginative and narrative play, they recruit and develop deeper levels of cognitive flexibility, self-monitoring, and focusing—as well as practice a variety of other cognitive processes, such as working memory. As a result, play in CCPT likely contributes to positive therapeutic outcomes in part because it creates a space in which children develop self-regulatory skills which, in turn, decrease emotional dysregulation and increase a sense of well-being.

A third reason for play's effectiveness is its cathartic properties. Catharsis is the release or discharge of emotion. In the context of CCPT, catharsis is most frequently related to emotions resulting from traumatic experiences.[43] Children who have experienced traumatic events, such as natural disasters, kidnapping, domestic violence, and abuse often reenact the events during play therapy.[44] Crucially, these reenactments occur in the safe context of the play-therapy office and the therapist's presence. Furthermore, the reenactments often involve slight modifications which emphasize the child's control instead of his powerlessness in the original traumatic situation. These two factors combine to foster in a child an increased sense of security and mastery over situations and emotions that were previously experienced as unsafe, uncontrollable, and overwhelming. As a result, a child's previously held unpleasant emotions related to their trauma are discharged and transformed into newer, more manageable states: "In the safety of the playroom, the child can verbally or physically express and release emotional tensions. . . . This termination of "unfinished business" prevents future emotional arousal."[45]

How Effective is CCPT?

The first meta-analysis of play therapy was conducted in 2001.[46] This meta-analysis reviewed 42 studies of play therapy. The results indicated that play therapy produced an effect size of 0.66, which indicates that play therapy had an effect size comparable to other forms of child psychotherapy. This finding is congruent with the "common-factors" psychotherapy research which supports the view that the type or technique of therapy is less important than factors that are common to all forms of psychotherapy, such as goal consensus, the therapeutic alliance, empathy, and expectations.[47]

Subsequent meta-analyses attempted to increase their scope and to include more recent and rigorous controlled studies. The largest meta-analysis of CCPT examined 93 controlled studies which identified treatment outcomes over a variety of domains, such as behavior, social adjustment and functioning, and self-concept.[48] In sum, this meta-analysis identified a mean effect size of 0.80—generally considered a large treatment effect.[49] Interestingly, and at odds with common-factors predictions, this meta-analysis identified significant differences in effect size between non-directive and directive play therapies. The mean effect size for non-directive play therapies was 0.92 while the mean effect size for directive play therapies was 0.71, which is a statistically significant difference. The authors of the meta-analysis argue that, at the least, their data supports the practice of CCPT and possibly suggests reasons to prefer CCPT over more directive therapies. Yet the authors note that there are some limitations to their meta-analysis, namely that some of the included studies lacked rigor and called for further research.

Subsequent meta-analyses have found less impressive results that are more congruent with the common-factors psychotherapy research. Two of the most recent meta-analyses identified effect sizes between 0.21 to 0.38[50] and 0.47.[51] When compared to previous meta-analyses, the significant decrease in the effect size was almost certainly the result of including studies with stricter methodology and more specific estimates of effect sizes. Nevertheless, while subsequent meta-analyses were unable to make a strict comparison between treatment types due to methodological reasons, their findings suggest that CCPT may provide superior treatment effects when compared to other forms of therapy and that it is at least as effective as other interventions (for example, behavioral therapy). CCPT research continues to expand, focusing on diverse populations, specific and comorbid diagnoses, and the mediators and moderators of change.[52]

The outcomes reviewed here suggest that CCPT has powerful effects on children's emotional states and behavior. These effects are important to consider when planning interventions to assist children who are experiencing distress or behavioral problems. This is especially true since there is a tendency to biologize children's distress and problematic behavior, resulting in a tendency to intervene with medication instead of psychosocial interventions such as CCPT. Now, I discuss the increasing trend in explaining distress and problematic behavior via biology, some reasons this tendency is clinically problematic, and how an approach that integrates CCPT and other psychosocial interventions can more comprehensively and humanely assist children.

Biologizing Distress and Problematic Behaviour

There is an increasing trend to seek primarily or exclusively biological explanations of distress and problematic behavior—a view that we will subsequently refer to as "biogenetic etiologies" of mental disorders. To illustrate this, consider that when the fifth edition of the *Diagnostic and Statistical Manual of Mental Disorders* (*DSM-5*) was published in 2013, many of its producers had mixed feelings about it. Many of those responsible for creating the *DSM-5* had hoped that neuroscience, genetics, and other biological sciences would significantly inform the diagnostic criteria.[53] Yet the *DSM-5* states that there are no x-rays, lab tests, or biomarkers for psychiatric disorders such as major depressive disorder (MDD), attention-deficit hyperactivity disorder (ADHD), generalized anxiety disorder (GAD), or any other psychiatric disorder.[54] In fact, Thomas Insel, the head of the National Institute of Mental Health (NIMH) until November 2015, lamented that researchers and clinicians have no clinically actionable biomarkers for any psychiatric disorder; even the biological markers *associated* with psychiatric disorders have seldom been replicable.[55]

Nevertheless, as it became increasingly clear that the *DSM-5* would not integrate biomarkers, the NIMH undertook a new research program: the Research Domain Criteria Project (RDoC).[56] Many factors motivated launching the RDoC.[57] One of the most important is that it appears that those responsible for the RDoC endorse a form of physicalism which implies that the brain is responsible for psychological experience and that, as a result, disordered psychological and behavioral function is the result of disordered brain function.[58]

This biogenetic thinking can be seen in studies that attempt to link divergent brain activity with psychiatric disorders. There are thousands of such studies. For example, one recent study found statistically significant results indicating that children and adolescents who have been diagnosed with ADHD, oppositional defiant disorder, and conduct disorder have, on average, smaller brain structure and reduced brain activity in brain areas such as the bilateral amygdala, bilateral insula, and right striatum.[59] The study's authors suggested that their findings will one day provide an integrated brain model which will both explain *and* suggest treatment of these disorders, such as giving stimulant medication to children who have reduced brain activity. The development of the RDoC has resulted in numerous articles identifying and raising concern regarding biogenetic etiologies, including the way in which they can potentially negatively impact research and clinical implications.[60] For example, one author worries that "investigators operating within the RDoC framework must be careful not to confuse biological mediation with biological etiology. . . . For example, in principle, a psychological condition could be triggered largely by psychosocial factors, such as childhood sexual or physical abuse. Although this condition would of course be mediated by brain circuitry, its etiology would be primarily environmental."[61] This author elsewhere claims that the RDoC's emphasis on disordered brains causing psychiatric problems is akin to placing an emphasis on gravity causing airplane crashes—true, but not informative.

Others worry that it is not presently possible, and may never be possible, to understand the complex, dynamic causal loops which exist between cognition, belief, brain function, and psychiatric problems.[62] Still others express concern that the RDoC is highly unlikely to succeed because of the irreducible social component of psychiatric disorders.[63] These concerns lead to deep questions in the philosophy of mind and the philosophy of science (which won't be answered here). Nevertheless, many scholars in the field have noted an increasing trend to rely on biogenetic etiologies in psychiatry.

Negative Consequences of Biogenetic Etiologies

Biogenetic etiologies may have significant, negative clinical implications. Two implications are reviewed here. First, consider the relationship between the emphasis on biogenetic etiologies and medication use. Numerous studies have found that the more mental health practitioners, mental health patients, and the public endorse a biogenetic etiology of psychiatric disorders, the more likely they are to endorse medication.[64] To illustrate this, consider ADHD, one of the most commonly diagnosed psychiatric disorders among children.[65] The Center for Disease Control (CDC) has identified that, despite newer recommendations that children should first be treated with psychological and/or social interventions, they are often immediately treated with ADHD medication[66] and, unfortunately, sometimes with antipsychotics.[67] "Brain differences" were listed as the cause of

ADHD by 92% of respondents, a far higher percentage than any other causal story, such as parenting (32%), low effort (23%), or stress (65%).[68] Research has shown that parents who believe less in psychological causes of ADHD are significantly more likely to treat their children with medication.[69] Another line of evidence supporting the increased preference for medication can be seen in cultural practices. For instance, in France, where understanding of childhood psychiatric disorders often more comprehensively integrates psychological and social information about children's context, only about .5% of children are diagnosed with ADHD *and* treated with medication.[70] This is significantly less than the 9% of children diagnosed with ADHD and treated with medication in the United States.[71]

This emphasis on medication is concerning.[72] Medications have a variety of negative side effects. For instance, a recent study identified that Ritalin—a common ADHD medication—significantly increases the risk of myocardial infarction and arrhythmias during the initial phases of treatment.[73] The study emphasizes that medication should be used only after alternative treatments have been considered. Many other studies have identified other adverse reactions to ADHD medication, such as loss of appetite, growth disruption (in height and weight), sleep disturbance, mood disruption, stomach pain, psychotic symptoms, and higher rates of adolescent and adult obesity.[74] In addition to these negative side effects, the long-term effects of ADHD medication are relatively unknown and may pose other serious risks.[75]

An Alternative

The negative consequences described above are especially worthy of consideration because there is general agreement that psychosocial interventions, such as CCPT and other therapies, are as effective as medication for many childhood and adolescent psychiatric disorders.[76] In addition, psychosocial interventions appear to account more comprehensively and humanely for the distress and disturbance of individuals. Consider, for instance, the emotional and behavioral problems experienced by many foster children. These children often come from troubled backgrounds and have fewer psychological, emotional, and financial resources available to them than others. Unfortunately, they are also medicated, often with powerful antipsychotics being used off-label and at high rates.[77] Is it not at least plausible that these children's distresses are caused by their challenging environments just as much as their brains? And if so, does it not make sense to first give children the option to improve via psychosocial techniques before introducing psychotropic medication which has a wide variety of adverse consequences?

While medications may be useful in controlling problematic symptoms, psychological approaches (such as CCPT) are also effective and they significantly avoid the adverse consequences of them. It is thus worth emphasizing the power and beneficial effects of Child-Centered Play Therapy to children (and their parents) who are experiencing psychiatric problems.

Chapter Two
Mental Disorders and Genetics

In 2015, Roberto A. Ferdman wrote an article for the *Washington Post* titled "Why you shouldn't blame yourself for binge eating." Long story short, Mr. Ferdman concluded, "The next time you find yourself in a rut, and eating too much, know that the unbecoming scene isn't merely a question of will power—it's rather, in all likelihood, a matter of your genetic makeup."[78] In other words, it is not *you*. Your agency is mostly irrelevant. Because your binge eating is a consequence of your genes—"a matter of your genetic makeup."

As mentioned in the previous chapter, biogenetic explanations of behavior are on the rise. One of the most prominent ways these explanations are presented is via the claim that mental disorders are, at least partially, caused by genetics. Despite the prevalence of this type of explanation, there are data which challenge this picture and I will be using Ferdman's binge eating article to highlight some of these data.

First, I briefly discuss the power of beliefs as well as some theory surrounding biogenetic explanations of mental disorders. Next, I examine the evidence Ferdman used to justify his claim that binge eating is caused by genetics. I discuss the study he referred to, some important methodological features involved in determining the genetic contribution to mental disorders, and some sociological features of behavioral genetics. What I want to show is that this article dramatically exaggerates the genetic contribution to binge eating and that this type of presentation likely has negative consequences for those struggling to overcome binge eating.

Significance

Ferdman's article has the potential to change what individuals believe about binge eating. Ferdman suggested to his readers that struggle with binge eating not to beat themselves up—at least not to the extent they have in the past. And they should not beat themselves up for binge eating because it is *not in their control*. Their genetics are causing the behavior. So even if those who binge eat cannot change their genetics, they can change how they evaluate their behavior.

There is much I admire about this approach. Centrally, Ferdman is pointing out that what individuals believe can have significant impacts on how they feel, think, and behave. If Ferdman is successful in changing what his readers believe about binge eating, this could powerfully change how they think of themselves. Maybe they will be less harsh on themselves. Since being harsh is often one of the most painful aspects of binge-eating, this could be an important source of relief.

Ferdman is right to emphasize the power of beliefs. For example, one important feature of cognitive-behavioral therapy (CBT), a well-studied and effective psychotherapy, is that individuals struggling with mental disorders often have a variety of troublesome beliefs that significantly contribute to their problems.[78] Nearly 50 years ago, psychological theories identified that individuals who experience clinical depression frequently hold a cluster of beliefs such as "I can't stand myself because" or "I'm no good" or "I'll never amount to anything."[79] It is not that these individuals consciously choose, day after day, to believe phrases like these. These beliefs are generally automatic—they are deeply rooted habits. Nevertheless, these beliefs can be changed with time and effort—and new, more positive, adaptive, and pleasant emotions tend to follow.

This leads to another set of beliefs: beliefs about prognosis. Research has shown that the greater an individual endorses biogenetic etiologies of mental disorders, the greater their prognostic pessimism. Thus, while an individual who endorses a genetic etiology of binge eating may be less harsh on themselves, they are also likely to believe they will participate in binge eating more frequently and for longer periods of time. Explaining to someone struggling with binge eating that their binge eating is "part of their genetic makeup" probably contributes to a belief along the lines of "this is just how I am" and implies that their binge eating will be unlikely to change.

Since an individual's actual prognosis is related to their expected prognosis—individuals who expect to do better, do better—this means individuals who endorse a biogenetic etiology of binge eating will likely binge eat more in addition to being less likely to seek psychotherapy.[80]

The Evidence

Regardless of the beliefs, what about the evidence that binge eating is caused by our genes? If it is the case that binge eating really is caused by genetic makeup, then the considerations above, though interesting, probably are not crucial.

In his article, Ferdman placed the entire weight of his assertion about genetics on one study by Racine et al.[81] In order to critically assess the article, it is important to understand how studies like Racine et al. attempt to show that genetic makeup is a contributing factor to a mental disorder. Before diving in, it should be noted that no study I have reviewed makes claims that genetics determine mental disorders in the way Ferdman suggested. Psychiatric genetic research is modest and only suggests a genetic contribution, not a genetic determinate.

For quite some time, psychiatric researchers have been trying to identify genes responsible for mental disorders. This process has, thus far, been disappointing. Researchers have struggled to find genes that are reliably associated with mental disorders.[82] As a result of these disappointments, psychiatric researchers often conduct genome-wide association studies (GWAS) to see if large sample sizes lead to the identification of clusters of genes that are significantly more common in individuals diagnosed with a mental disorder than in those not diagnosed. It is not uncommon for researchers to identify statistically significant findings. However, these findings almost always fail to replicate. Even if they did, the increased risk of psychological disorders related to the cluster of genes, although statistically significant (unlikely to be due to chance), does not make a significant real-world impact. In other words, although a collection of genes may be associated with a mental disorder such as binge eating, having that collection of genes does not guarantee binge eating and only slightly increases the risk.

To illustrate what I mean, consider that large GWAS studies on schizophrenia—the mental disorder with the strongest evidence for being a genuine biological disease (though even this evidence is surprisingly weak)—are only able to identify genes which account for "1.1% of the absolute risk" of an individual being diagnosed with schizophrenia.[83]

There is even less evidence for a genetic contribution to other mental disorders. For example, Ripke et al. described how, though the authors conducted the largest ever GWAS of major depression, they were "unable to identify robust and replicable" genetic markers.[84]

Although GWAS have not been very successful, researchers persist, arguing that more research will eventually make real gains. To understand why researchers maintain hope despite disappointing results, it is important to understand the influence of twin studies in motivating genetic research. It is commonly thought that twin studies suggest a genetic component of mental disorders. For example, the classical twin method compares concordance rates—if one, both, or neither twin is diagnosed with the same mental disorder—between identical twins (monozygotic twins [MZ]) and fraternal twins (dizygotic twins [DZ]). MZ twins share 100% of the same genes. DZ twins share about 50% of the same genes. Crucially, twins in many types of twin studies are raised in the same environment. So, if it turns out that MZ twins reliably have higher concordance rates of, for example, binge eating, than DZ twins, then this would seem to count as evidence that there is a genetic component to binge eating. In other words, if twins who share 100% of the same genes as well as the same environment are more concordant than twins who share 50% of the same genes as well as the same environment, then a plausible explanation of the elevated rates of concordance is the higher level of genetic similarity.

Even if we grant all of this, the language of Ferdman's article is misleading because even the Racine et al. study results show that there is nowhere near a perfect concordance rate between MZ twins.[85] Less than half of MZ twins both participate in binge eating. In other words, it is common for one of the MZ twin pair to binge eat while the other twin does not. If genetic makeup is causing binge eating, why are twins with 100% of the same genes not having 100% of the same binge eating rates? There is no question that any sort of genetic deterministic claim from Ferdman overstates even his own evidence.

Nevertheless, the Racine et al. study does seem to show that MZ twins have higher concordance rates for a variety of psychological features, including binge eating, than DZ twins.[86] So, although it is clear we should reject Ferdman's stronger claim—that genes determine binge eating—we could adopt a weaker claim that genes somehow contribute to binge eating.

At the same time, even this weak claim for genetic contribution has been challenged. The central assumption of the classical twin method is that MZ and DZ twins share an equal environment.[87] At first glance, this seems straightforward. In the relevant studies, both the MZ and the DZ twins are raised in the same household—so it is close to a brute fact that they share equal environments.

However, decades ago it was argued that MZ twins share a more similar environment than DZ twins. MZ twins have an "ego fusion" that is greater than DZ twins. That is, they are treated more alike, found together more often, and share more similar experiences. In short, MZ twins have a more similar environment than DZ twins, and thus it could be the more similar environment causing the more similar concordance rates.

Jackson provided support for this argument in several ways.[88] For example, he pointed out that female MZ twins were consistently more concordant than male MZ twins. This high concordance level could not be because of genetic factors—whether male or female, MZ twins have the same genetic makeup. So, what might cause the greater concordance rate? A variety of environmental factors, such as the fact that females (at that time) may have shared more similar environments because of being kept indoors more often than males and increased female closeness being more accepted than male closeness.

A similar line of reasoning applies to the numerous other identifications[89]: that DZ twins were more concordant than siblings (despite the fact that DZ twins and siblings share approximately the same level of genetic similarity); that female DZ twins were more concordant than male DZ twins; and that same-sex DZ twins had higher concordance than opposite-sex DZ twins.[90] In each of these observations, the genetic hypothesis cannot explain the higher concordance rate while the environmental hypothesis has, at least, a plausible chance to.[91]

But if the argument against the equal environment assumption is strong, why do genetic accounts of mental disorders continue to be so popular? Aaron Panofsky provides, I think, a good working hypothesis.[92] He provided a detailed account of the history of behavioral genetics and its prominent advocates. In that history, he explained that the behavioral geneticists "main techniques for demonstrating genetic influences on behavior—twin and adoption studies and the estimation of heritability—had been criticized and undermined from seemingly every possible angle" and that they had not produced adequate answers to these criticisms.[93] This prompted him to ask:

Facing these conditions, how could behavior geneticists promote genetics in psychology—the field from which most hailed—and other behavioral sciences? . . . [They] turned their weaknesses into strengths . . . They directed their attentions outward, seeking attention and recognition . . . [They] made it possible to use their tools without having to join their field or assume their identity. They accumulated findings that gave behavior genetics an imprimatur of scientific successes without addressing the fundamental critiques. Indeed, to this day the basic premises of behavior genetics' claims and techniques are still controversial across the sciences...[94]

In other words, behavioral geneticists' general response to the methodological criticism of their work was to complete more and more research which could be integrated with more and more disciplines. The breadth of their work covers the lack of depth associated with the methodological problems of the discipline.

Concluding Thoughts

Concretely, you would not know these types of problems existed by reading Ferdman.[95] What you would learn from him is that binge eating is a result of your genetic makeup.

I think at least one of the factors involved here is that medical science has been remarkably successful in treating medical conditions, and we would like that success to translate into increased understanding and treatment of mental disorders. After all, many believe that human beings are, fundamentally, biological entities and so it makes sense to try and find biological causes for our mental disorders. I'm sure that biological research can inform our understanding of mental disorders, but I think it is unlikely biological findings will ever explain them.

Chapter Three
Mental Disorders and Brain Scan Research

Recently, there have been intense debates and controversies within the mental health field regarding the validity of the current diagnostic system, how to best work with individuals in distress, and what constitutes "mental illness." The British Psychological Society[96] and the International Society for Ethical Psychology and Psychiatry[97] have both issued statements asserting that "mental illnesses" are best conceptualized as problems in living that result from traumatic and societal ills which overwhelm one's capacity to cope and that "treatment" should be based in a psychosocial framework that honors individuality. On the other hand, the mainstream mental health field—particularly biological psychiatry—in conjunction with various political and corporate powers, is pushing further in the direction of conceiving emotional distress as a brain disease; a direction often referred to as "biological reductionism."

Advocates of biological psychiatry are calling for more brain science and a shift from a system of many discrete mental disorders based on a list of symptoms to a system that retains the framework of discrete mental disorders but shifts the diagnostic criteria to differentiations within brain activity and/or brain structure. Conversely, others have come to believe that applying further funding and resources toward strengthening a disease-based diagnostic system of "mental illnesses," (i.e., the "medical model") rather than psychosocial interventions and prevention methods, is profoundly misguided and potentially detrimental to the vulnerable individuals that mental health professionals are purportedly trying to help.

As alluded to in Chapter One, much of this controversy began with the newest edition of the *Diagnostic and Statistical Manual of Mental Disorders,* the *DSM-5.*[98] This greatly expanded version of the *DSM* is the latest in a series of ongoing revisions to a diagnostic system that has emerged from a tremendous effort spanning more than 150 years to classify and categorize human distress. Controversially, at the time of the *DSM-5*'s release in April 2013, Thomas Insel, then the director of the National Institute of Mental Health (NIMH), released a statement saying that the *DSM*'s "weakness is its lack of validity" and that "patients with mental disorders deserve better." This was part of an announcement proclaiming a shift in funding research supported by the NIMH to be centered on the Research Domain Criteria (RDoC). This is proposed to "transform diagnosis by incorporating genetics, imaging, cognitive science, and other levels of information to lay the foundation for a new classification system . . . not constrained by the current *DSM* categories."[99] The Chairman of the *DSM-5* responded, "We've been telling patients for several decades that we are waiting for biomarkers. We're still waiting."[100] This statement by Dr. Kupfer strongly questions the continued narrow focus on—thus far—nonexistent biomarkers, particularly when it is done so at the expense of other frameworks, even if those approaches (i.e., the *DSM*) are flawed.

These events show a powerful movement toward a new system of mental disorder diagnoses based on biomarkers and brain scans that follows in the footsteps of traditional medical diagnoses. This line of research has been promoted as an exciting step toward a more scientifically advanced understanding of human suffering and behavior.

The motivation driving this movement is understandable. Many people experience severe forms of distress, torment, and disability. It is also clear that the current system is doing a poor job of adequately addressing this problem. The hope for many is that a brain-based approach will provide a more evidence-based understanding of these disorders. Furthermore, a brain-based approach to sometimes difficult-to-understand behaviors and experiences of those in extreme distress may be a way to explain distress without blaming anybody or insisting that someone "just get over it." By attributing "mental illness" to biology, it may be thought that stigma surrounding mental health difficulties may be reduced. In addition, brain-based accounts of mental illness could allow for the creation of more effective psychopharmacological treatments and identification of those who have the most need for our limited resources. Finally, when professionals charge insurance companies and federal agencies for reimbursement for services rendered, people want to know that the money is being spent effectively.

The problem with this approach, however, is that the brain-based initiatives for clinical research rely on a disease model that is based on questionable logic, a faulty, reductionistic view of human nature, and it contradicts many of the most robust research findings. Much of the brain research conducted thus far appears to indicate that most of the conditions referred to as mental illnesses are likely otherwise healthy adaptive processes in response to extreme environmental experiences. Although it appears that such adaptive processes often do correlate with changes within the brain and that they may lead to certain long-term problems for the individual, these changes do not necessarily signify biological disease. Furthermore, brain research has reinforced the benefits of certain psychosocial interventions, such as yoga, meditation, and psychotherapy, thereby negating the assumption that the resolution of such distressing conditions requires psychopharmacological or other related biological interventions.

Despite the robust evidence pointing to the importance of psychosocial factors in both the onset and the resolution of distressing psychological conditions, we find the mainstream mental health field continuing to emphasize biologically based research while increasingly neglecting psychosocial research and support. Although it may at first appear counterintuitive that the field continues down a path that contradicts much of the recovery research, the reasoning for it seems to become clearer if we keep these points in mind: This path is strongly encouraged by powerful vested interests,[101] people are suffering, and we want answers that are unambiguous and easily implemented. Regardless of the reasoning, the fact remains that in spite of the great technological advances within the emerging brain-based initiatives, because they retain the same flawed core assumptions that gave rise to the *DSM* system—particularly conflating psychological distress and/or brain anomalies with biological disease—it is likely that they will leave us with little more than the further entrenchment of these flawed assumptions to the detriment of many. So, although the ongoing research of neurological and genetic correlates of psychological distress may be valuable as an academic exercise, we fear the consequences.

Current Findings and Flawed Assumptions

The last several decades have seen hundreds of studies reporting discoveries correlating brain activity with human emotion, behavior, and experience. However, the consensus is that there has yet to be any replicable findings that show distinct differences or abnormalities associated with any *DSM* category, as evidenced by this statement by Thomas Insel: "We cannot design a system based on biomarkers or cognitive performance because we lack the data . . . . This is what we have been doing for decades when we reject a biomarker because it does not detect a *DSM* category."[102] Although reports continue to be published suggesting associations between particular brain activity and specific disorders, these fail to hold significance when looked at in the aggregate across diagnostic categories. Furthermore, such findings fail to delineate between those individuals who have experienced trauma and chronic stress—particularly childhood trauma—but who do not have clinically significant symptoms and those who are significantly disabled by such distressing conditions.

For instance, it is often said that schizophrenia is known to be a debilitating, lifelong, brain-based disease. Studies show significantly reduced brain volume in particular areas of the brain in individuals diagnosed with schizophrenia.[103] However, these same abnormalities are also shown more generally to be directly associated with severe stress in early childhood,[104] severe emotional deprivation in early childhood,[105] and/or chronic social stress and discrimination.[106] In addition, it has been known for some time by researchers that many studies indicating a reduced brain volume show that this is directly caused by the effects of antipsychotic drugs.[107] Undermining the brain-disease assumption even further are studies in which brain scans of children diagnosed with schizophrenia show similar abnormalities as their healthy siblings; as adults, those diagnosed with schizophrenia still have similar brain abnormalities, whereas their non-diagnosed siblings went on to have "normal" brain scans as adults.[108] This shows not only that the structure of the brain can change for various reasons over time but also that abnormalities in the brain do not necessarily equate with abnormal behavior. Rather, there is likely some other shared variable involved with types of psychological distress, such as the home in which these siblings were raised.

A similar pattern of brain anomalies and changes associated with environmental and psychotropic influences can be found for other diagnostic categories thought to be brain-based diseases, such as attention deficit/hyperactivity disorder (ADHD) and depression. The reason for this pattern of findings is that brain activity appears to be most closely associated with certain subjective phenomena, for instance: hearing voices, seeing visions, impulsivity, fatigue, and so forth, that do not uniquely map onto *DSM*-defined categories and are associated with various environmental influences.

Many studies have suggested a link between inflammation and serious emotional distress,[109] yet inflammation is known to be a direct result of chronic stress and/or poor diet. Furthermore, chronic stress and trauma have been found to not only change the structure and activity of the brain,[110] but that of gene expression as well.[111] In fact, the most consistent finding across all diagnostic categories is abnormalities in the hypothalamic-pituitary-adrenal (HPA) axis, which is an area of the brain that is specifically associated with trauma and stress.[112] Although many tend to take for granted that posttraumatic stress disorder (PTSD) is the only syndrome directly caused by traumatic events, we cannot say that trauma has any more direct causal link with PTSD than it does with other phenomena such as hyperactivity, psychosis, or depression.[113] To conflate distressing experiences and the body's natural reaction to such experiences with biological disease is a giant leap in logic and could also result in minimization and denial of the traumatic and stressful experiences that initially led to the emotional distress.

In the same way that the environment may negatively affect the structure of the brain, so too may there be positive influences. Training that involves the active participation of parents has been shown to change the brains of children who are diagnosed with ADHD,[114] whereas psychotherapy, in general, has been shown to be associated with changes in the brain consistent with changes in behavior.[115] In addition to more formal psychotherapeutic intervention, other healthy practices have also been shown to have a direct effect on the brain. For instance, meditation has been shown to increase brain volume in as little as 8 weeks,[116] aerobic exercise can increase the volume in an area of the brain directly associated with the effects of trauma,[117] and eating healthily may reverse brain abnormalities associated with addiction to food.[118]

This research seems to show that the brain adapts to its environment. In fact, one could even interpret the findings of many of the brain differences in traumatized and distressed individuals as signs of adaptive functioning—the opposite of disease.

In summary, the only consistent and replicable findings in brain-based mental health research have been those showing the relationship of early childhood stress, neglect, trauma, poor diet, and/or lack of exercise on the structure and neural connectivity within the brain. Similar brain abnormalities can be identified in siblings where one sibling has been diagnosed with a psychological disorder and the other has never shown any sign of psychological dysfunction. This alone should make people question the utility of assuming biological disease based simply on brain differences. In addition, healthy behaviors and psychotherapeutic interventions have significant and measurable effects on the brain, further underscoring the importance of understanding environmental effects on developing children and of intervening at familial and systemic levels. At this time, there is no evidence of any disease process in any of the so-called mental disorders, except that which is associated with the long-term use of medications.[119]

Consequences of the Continued Search for "Disease" in the Brain

There are at least two prominent negative consequences of focusing on biological, brain-based etiologies of mental illness: skewed research funding and biased treatment preferences. Biologically focused research programs problematically skew research funding. Although brain-based research has received a vastly disproportionate share of mental health funding, there have been little to no advancements in symptom or functional outcomes for individuals diagnosed with serious mental illness within the biological/disease model. This leads us to question the logic of continuing to fund this line of research, particularly when it is at the expense of alternative theories. A. Frances described this funding/research situation as follows:

NIMH was at the center of the neuroscience enthusiasm, dubbing the 1990s the "decade of the brain" and betting the house on a narrow biological agenda to replace what previously had been a more balanced portfolio of research into not only the basic sciences, but also into treatments and health services. In effect, NIMH turned itself into a "brain institute" rather than an "institute of mental health."

Its efforts have succeeded in producing wonderful science, but have failed in helping patients.[120]

This problem will likely become more prevalent as the RDoC gains momentum. Frances worried that the RDoC "will almost certainly deliver nothing of practical import within this decade. My guess is that it will consist of a slow, steady slog of tiny steps, more characterized by frustrating blind alleys than by any great leaps forward."[121] This was echoed by Phillips, who argued:

> The RDoC initiative, though intellectually appealing (to neuroscientists), is tone deaf to the current global trajectory of mental health. . . . This high-profile focus of NIMH funding on the very long-term goal of establishing biologically-based diagnostic categories . . . may ultimately prove impossible for a substantial proportion of the persons we currently treat.[122]

Second, biologically focused research can skew treatment preferences. Emphasizing biological, reductionistic etiologies of mental illness prejudices clinicians and patients to believe medication is the most effective form of treatment.[123] Although medication may sometimes be useful, it also has a variety of negative side effects, some of which can be extremely serious. For example, some of the side effects of antidepressants include increased risk of relapse after discontinuation, negative effects on attention, a variety of gastrointestinal problems, disruption of the blood clotting process and abnormal bleeding, impaired sexual functioning, and some evidence of negative effects on embryos and fetuses in pregnant women consuming antidepressants.[124] Some of the negative side effects of antipsychotics include irreversible alterations in brain size, structure, and function; tardive dyskinesia; obesity and associated conditions such as diabetes, heart disease, and stroke; and other cardiovascular problems.[125] In other words, many of the biological anomalies that one finds with chronic sufferers of mental illness are caused by the biological interventions thought necessary to decrease distress.

There is also an increase in research demonstrating the severe and prolonged symptoms of withdrawal from these drugs.[126] Often, when people choose to discontinue the use of these addictive substances, the changes in their brains can lead to supersensitivity to particular experiences.[127] So, for instance, when one desires to stop taking an antipsychotic that has been prescribed long-term, and the person does not taper slowly, the person is particularly likely to experience a kind of rebound psychosis. This withdrawal effect of brain-altering drugs is then taken as proof that the drugs were necessary, and that the person does, in fact, have a biological disease.[128] This circular reasoning, which is not based in scientific long-term research, can trap a person in a lifelong cycle of extreme distress and disability.

Critically, many studies have found treatment alternatives to medication are effective. For example, evidence suggests that psychotherapy is as effective as antidepressant medication or as psychotherapy plus antidepressant medication for the treatment of depression.[129] Recent longitudinal research has also shown that those who do not take antipsychotic medication long-term have better outcomes than those who remain on these drugs continuously.[130] In short, evidence suggests that although many drugs may provide temporary relief, underlying societal factors, psychosocial factors, environmental factors problems in living must be acknowledged and addressed to gain increased quality of life and functional recovery.

Concluding Thoughts and Discussion

Having reviewed the relevant research and having considered the pros and cons of the general trend of devoting increasing resources toward seeking the etiologies and remedies for psychological distress within the brain, we conclude that this trend is problematic and misguided. Attempts to arrive at a biologically based diagnostic system for those conditions of human distress not clearly associated with a genuine medical condition (so-called mental illnesses) have so far been costly and relatively unsuccessful. Biological interventions for such conditions have consistently been associated with more detrimental long-term outcomes and increased chronicity of distress.

Poverty, trauma, child abuse and neglect, discrimination, loneliness, bullying, drug use, and inequality are directly associated with such conditions and are also correlated with certain kinds of observable changes within our brains. Psychosocial support that directly addresses these issues has been consistently associated with long-term benefits superior to those of biological interventions. We need to acknowledge that the resources available for mental health research and care are limited and that every dollar and hour spent pursuing brain-based solutions to psychological distress comes at a direct cost to those resources available for psychosocial research and support.

This is no easy task, to be sure, but if we honestly want to ask the question, "What causes mental illness, and how do we best treat it?" then we need to be willing to look honestly at the research and accept the answers that emerge.

Chapter 4
Depression and the Chemical Imbalance Hypothesis

In 2006, 80% of Americans agreed with the claim that a chemical imbalance within the brain is a cause of depression. This figure of 80% was a more than 10-point increase over the past 10 years.[131] Powered by philosophic argument, scientific evidence, and multi-million-dollar advertising campaigns, the chemical imbalance hypothesis has saturated our academic and popular culture.[132] This saturation is at least partially responsible for more than 10 billion dollars annually spent on antidepressant medication in the United States. But what is the chemical imbalance hypothesis? And what evidence supports it? This chapter provides an account of the chemical imbalance hypothesis, a history of its development, and the evidence provided for its justification. It will show that the evidence for the chemical imbalance hypothesis is unconvincing, and it will discuss why, despite the unconvincing evidence, the hypothesis lingers.

What Is the Chemical Imbalance Hypothesis of Depression?

The chemical imbalance hypothesis of depression is the theory that individuals diagnosed with depression experience their depression because of disordered brain function. The brain is responsible for regulating an enormous amount of function and behavior. An essential element involved in this process is the transmission of signals throughout the brain. It transmits these signals through neurons. Recent estimates suggest that the brain has around 86 billion neurons.[133] These neurons transmit signals to one another across the space between them—the synapses. In most cases, neurons affect one another via chemicals stored within them, called neurotransmitters, which are released into the synapse. After the neurotransmitters are released, one of three things will happen to them: (1) They are destroyed in the synapse by enzymes, (2) they are captured by the neuron that sent them (reuptake), or (3) they maintain their position in the synapse. There are several types of neurotransmitters. Some prominent examples are dopamine, serotonin, and norepinephrine. The chemical imbalance hypothesis is that there is a deficiency in one or more of these neurotransmitters.[134]

The "Discovery" of Antidepressants

The idea that depression is caused by a chemical imbalance originated from observations from two complimentary directions. The first was that some drugs, which increased the levels of neurotransmitters available, seemed to lessen the depression experienced by those who took them.[135] The second was that the drug reserpine, which reduced the levels of neurotransmitters available, seemed to induce depression in those who took it.[136] We will briefly examine the history of both directions in turn.

Healy detailed that the first two antidepressant drugs (though they weren't called "antidepressants") were iproniazid and imipramine.[137] Iproniazid was first used to treat tuberculosis and was not developed as a psychiatric drug.[138] However, during its administration, clinicians noted that some of the patients given iproniazid experienced a boost in energy. These reports were notable enough that, in 1957, Loomer, Saunders, and Kline from the Rockland State Hospital conducted the first well-known evaluation of iproniazid as a "psychic energizer."[139] Unlike typical stimulants, psychic energizers acted selectively. This meant that they did not significantly stimulate motor function and general cerebral activity but, instead, targeted an individual's affective state.[140] In their report, Loomer et al. documented that about two-thirds of the patients they treated with iproniazid presented "varying degrees of improvement" while taking the drug.[141] Their study did not include a placebo control group. Nevertheless, this trial run of iproniazid was influential and sparked more interest and research in the drug.[142] Less than a year after Loomer et al. was published, "more than 400,000 depressed patients had been treated with iproniazid."[143]

Around a year after the iproniazid study mentioned was complete, the psychiatrist Roland Kuhn published an article on the drug imipramine in *The American Journal of Psychiatry*.[144] Like iproniazid, imipramine was not initially designed as an antidepressant. It was originally intended to help manage psychosis. However, as Kuhn was using imipramine to help his patients with psychotic symptoms, he noticed that several of them seemed to have a significant lessening of their depressive symptoms. Kuhn claimed that a high percentage of patients treated with imipramine achieved "full or social recovery" and that the side effects of the drug were "relatively slight."[145] About a year before, Kuhn had presented data on imipramine at the International Congress of Psychiatry. Even though previous drug treatments of depression had been, more or less, universally ineffective, Kuhn's presentation on imipramine aroused interest.[146] By 1959, numerous trials of imipramine had been conducted.[147]

The interest in these new drugs was significant, and a new concept for them emerged. Moncrieff detailed how, in 1958, the term *antidepressant* was virtually unused in academic papers published (in a search of MEDLINE).[148] However, in 1959, more than 100 published papers included *antidepressant*, which indicates a substantial rise in the interest and discussion of the term. At least two lines of reasoning were influential in this interest. First, the importance of the placebo effect was not widely understood at the time. Thus, when individuals were given a drug and, subsequently, they demonstrated improvement, the general conclusion was that improvement was because of a drug effect on its own. Second, psychiatrists of the time possessed a tremendous desire to find biological, brain-based causes for psychological disorders.[149]

This desire had a pivotal manifestation in 1965.[150] During this year, Schildkraut argued that depression could be caused by too little norepinephrine in the synapses.[151] Two years later, Coppen argued along similar lines that depression could be caused by too little serotonin in the synapses.[152] In both of these articles, the justification for the claims that norepinephrine or serotonin deficiencies cause depression was twofold: First, drugs that increase the availability of particular neurotransmitters, such as iproniazid and imipramine, seem to alleviate the symptoms of depression. Second, reserpine, a drug that decreases the availability of neurotransmitters, seems to induce depression in individuals treated with it.

The inclusion of reserpine's effects in these papers is important because it provided a second, complimentary line of evidence supporting the chemical imbalance hypothesis. Reserpine was a drug initially explored in the treatment of hypertension.[153] In the course of studies examining reserpine's effect on hypertension, multiple independent researchers began documenting its apparent depressive effects.[154]

Also in the mid-1950s, it was discovered that reserpine reduced serotonin levels.[155]

By combining the data from the effects of iproniazid, imipramine, and reserpine, the stage was set for a fleshed out chemical imbalance hypothesis. The basic argument of the chemical imbalance hypothesis is that drugs "like reserpine that decrease monoamine neurotransmitters make people depressed. Drugs that increase these neurotransmitters by one means or another relieve their depression. Hence, depression is due to a [chemical imbalance]."[156]

The Evidence for the Chemical Imbalance Hypothesis of Depression

From the research examined so far, the conclusion was that iproniazid and imipramine increase neurotransmitter levels, and they also alleviate depression. Reserpine decreases neurotransmitter levels and is depressogenic. So, these data fit nicely together when justifying the claim that a chemical imbalance is causally related to depression.

However, these claims are not what they seem to be. Recall that "most of the evidence [for the chemical imbalance hypothesis] is indirect, deriving from pharmacological studies with drugs such as reserpine . . . and antidepressants which produce affective changes."[157] If this is true, and if it is the case that these drugs did not produce the purported affective changes, then the evidence the chemical imbalance hypothesis is based on would dissipate. This is precisely what multiple prominent researchers have argued by addressing both directions of the chemical imbalance hypothesis.[158]

Furthermore, over and beyond the challenges to the affective changes produced by these drugs, it is important to keep in mind that even if the evidence demonstrated that, for example, antidepressants do treat the symptoms of depression in a clinically significant manner, this would not demonstrate that the chemical imbalance hypothesis is correct. Aspirin treats the symptoms of headaches by blocking chemical reactions. This does not mean that aspirin treats the underlying etiology of the headache, such as a food allergies or stress.

Continuing pharmacological research may discover drugs that can reliably treat symptoms of depression. Like aspirin, such chemicals could treat symptoms without treating an underlying chemical imbalance. The potentially negative consequences of this potent form of chemical manipulation have been raised before and should be kept in mind as we bravely move forward.[159]

Nevertheless, examining the purported affective changes produced by these drugs is still worth undertaking. Therefore, we will now examine more detailed research on changes in neurotransmitter levels and depression.

Decreasing Neurotransmitters and Depression

The first direction of evidence provided for the chemical imbalance hypothesis is that drugs that decrease neurotransmitters cause depression. In the past, this was based on the understanding that certain drugs decreased neurotransmitters combined with clinical observations about mood and affect. Reserpine was the prime example.

To investigate this aspect of the chemical imbalance hypothesis, contemporary researchers have investigated "more direct evidence" of the relationship between decreased neurotransmitters and depression.[160] For example, when consumed, alpha-methyl-para-tyrosine and para-chlorophenylalanine cause a decrease in the availability of dopamine and serotonin.[161] Thus, if the chemical imbalance hypothesis is right, administration of alpha-methyl-para-tyrosine or para-chlorophenylalanine should induce depression via decreased neurotransmitter levels. However, some time ago, it was shown that administration of alpha-methyl-para-tyrosine or para-chlorophenylalanine does not cause depression.[162] The underlying concept of the study by Mendels and Frazer—inducing a depletion of neurotransmitters and documenting affective change—has been repeated nearly 100 times.[163] Ruhé, Mason, and Schene conducted a meta-analysis on these depletion studies and found that a decrease in the availability of serotonin, norepinephrine, and dopamine "does not decrease mood in healthy controls" and that although:

> [. . .] previously the monoamine systems were considered to be responsible for the development of major depressive disorder,

the available evidence to date does not support a direct causal relationship with major depressive disorder. There is no simple direct correlation of 5-HT (serotonin) or NE (norepinephrine) levels in the brain and mood.[164]

How does this make sense? In the past, it was argued that reserpine, which was known to decrease neurotransmitter availability, was depressogenic. Reserpine is considered the "classic example" of a depressogenic drug.[165] This idea is cited in biological psychology textbooks.[166] So why is it that reserpine administration, which decreases neurotransmitter availability, induces depression, but alpha-methyl-para-tyrosine or para-chlorophenylalanine administration, which also decrease neurotransmitter availability, do not induce depression?

The answer provided to this question by Healy and Savage and Baumeister et al. is that reserpine was never depressogenic to begin with.[167] Healy and Savage argued that "considering the evidence now, it is difficult to sustain a case that reserpine causes depression."[168] They made this argument after examining several studies, which closely tracked the effects of reserpine. These studies relied on rigorous controls and documentation instead of the clinical observations initially used to support reserpine's depressive effect. In these studies, reserpine was found not to induce depression. Thus, they argued, "There is a notion that in some way antidepressants act to increase amine levels. This would seem to need revision."[169] In short, they argued that the widespread idea that reserpine induces depression is contradicted by the evidence.

Baumeister et al. argued along similar lines.[170] They agreed with Healy and Savage, noting that "for nearly 50 years, the monoamine hypothesis has been the leading theory about the neuropathologic processes that underlie depression."[171] However, despite the fact that they agreed with both Healy and Valenstein regarding their conclusions about reserpine,[172] they claimed that "the writings of Healy and Valenstein on this topic have not included a thorough and systematic review of the literature."[173] So, the authors undertook the systematic review. In that review, they examined the case reports and the group studies that were used as evidence of reserpine's depressogenic effects. They concluded that:

> The present review indicates that there has never been a good reason to believe that reserpine is depressogenic. Nevertheless, this belief continues to be widely promoted as established fact. The question that this raises is why the scientific and medical community would hold onto a belief so tenaciously in the face of evidence to the contrary. A plausible explanation is that this belief provides essential support for the monoamine hypothesis of depression.[174]

The response—really, the lack of a response—to Baumeister et al.[175] is telling: according to a Google Scholar search, not one scholarly article has been published which criticizes their findings, although Nabeshima and Kim[176] cite Healy and Savage[177] and Baumeister et al.[178] *in support* of the claim that reserpine is depressogenic. And the reason for this, at least according to the authors, is that once you look beyond the myth of reserpine-induced depression to the observed facts related to its administration, the evidence overwhelmingly demonstrates that reserpine is not depressogenic.

Even stranger, and perhaps even more damaging to the chemical imbalance hypothesis, is that a popular antidepressant drug is not a selective serotonin reuptake inhibitor (SSRI) but a selective serotonin reuptake enhancer (SSRE).[179] The drug tianeptine is an SSRE. "Tianeptine's mechanism of action ostensibly defies logic as it enhances rather than inhibits reuptake of serotonin."[180] Kirsch expounds on this idea, noting that:

> If the monoamine imbalance theory is right, tianeptine ought to induce depression . . . but the clinical-trial data show . . . the opposite. . . . In head-to-head comparisons, of tianeptine with SSRIs and . . . tricyclic antidepressants, all three produced virtually identical response rates.[181]

So, the idea that a depletion of neurotransmitters—caused by substances such as alpha-methyl-para-tyrosine or para-chlorophenylalanine or by drugs such as reserpine or tianeptine—was thought to lend support to the chemical imbalance hypothesis. However, a closer examination of the data strongly—probably decisively—suggests that the chemical imbalance hypothesis, on this point, does not match the data.

Increasing Neurotransmitters and Depression

Recall that the chemical imbalance hypothesis originally relied on the idea that reserpine induced depression and drugs such as iproniazid and imipramine treat depression. So, even if it is the case that a reduction of neurotransmitters does not induce depression, it could still be, somehow, that an increase in neurotransmitters alleviates depression. And the effectiveness of contemporary antidepressant medication demonstrates just that. But does it?

New antidepressant drugs, such as SSRIs, seem to be remarkably effective at treating depression. The efficacy of SSRIs lends further evidence to the chemical imbalance hypothesis, even if it is true that depletion on neurotransmitters does not induce depression. But just how effective are SSRIs and other antidepressants?

For almost two decades, Irving Kirsch (Harvard) has spearheaded research that calls into question the efficacy of antidepressants and, subsequently, the validity of the chemical imbalance hypothesis. Kirsch argued that the data indicate that antidepressants offer only a small, clinically insignificant difference in treating depression when compared to placebos.[182] How could Kirsch make this argument in the face of patients who claim antidepressants work, psychiatrists arguing that antidepressants work, and research suggesting that antidepressants work?

His work began in 1995.[183] Up until that point, Kirsch had primarily been interested in researching the placebo effect—an area of study in which he is an expert and leading figure.[184] He was fascinated by the power that expectation, a key ingredient in the placebo effect, had on human experience.[185] He studied the placebo effect in various areas such as medication, hypnosis, and surgery.[186]

Coming from this background, it was only a matter of time, for at least two reasons, before Kirsch turned to the examination of antidepressants. First, antidepressants are a widely prescribed medication and, thus, a ripe target for anyone interested in studying the placebo effect on a grand scale. Second, "hopelessness is a central feature of depression [and] hope lies at the core of the placebo effect . . . . when the promise of relief instills hope, it counters a fundamental attribute of depression" and, thus, studying antidepressant medication offers a unique area of study in which expectancy and hope are critically important to treatment outcomes.[187]

In 1998, Kirsch and Sapirstein published the results of their meta-analysis documenting the placebo effect in those taking antidepressants. In this meta-analysis, they examined 38 clinical trials, which included thousands of depressed patients. This meta-analysis compared the improvement of patients when they were assigned to antidepressant medication, placebo, psychotherapy, or no treatment.[188] Within their meta-analysis, they found, "Although the drug effect in the published clinical trials that we had analyzed was statistically significant, it was much smaller than we had anticipated. Much of the therapeutic response to the drug was due to the placebo effect."[189]

Subsequently, Kirsch stated that he and Sapirstein were deeply confused by these results. After all, antidepressant medications "had been heralded as a revolution in the treatment of depression— blockbuster drugs that have been prescribed to hundreds of millions of patients, with annual sales totaling billions."[190] And yet, their meta-analysis seemed to show that these drugs were not having much of an effect over and beyond the placebo effect. They concluded that their meta-analysis must not be a comprehensive picture of the efficacy of antidepressants, and so they began to try and track down where they went wrong.

One of the first thoughts they had about the surprising results of their meta-analysis was that perhaps the type of antidepressant used, and the possible varying efficacy of each type, was responsible for the relatively dismal performance of antidepressant drugs when compared to placebo. Perhaps some low-performing antidepressants were dragging down other higher performing ones. When they dove back into the data, Kirsch and Sapirstein found that "some of these trials had assessed tricyclic antidepressants . . . . In other trials, the focus was on SSRIs like Prozac."[191] So, perhaps it was, after all, the type of antidepressant used that was a key feature of their findings.

However, when they examined the data after accounting for the diverse types of drugs used, they discovered that "not only did all of these medications produce the same degree of improvement in depression, but also, in each case, only 25 percent of the improvement was due to the effect of the drug."[192] And this wasn't the only interesting result of their more refined look at the drug type. Kirsch detailed that some of the medications included in the meta-analysis were not even antidepressants. Some of the studies included in the meta-analysis had included patients being given barbiturates, benzodiazepines, and even a synthetic thyroid hormone. Kirsch noted, "Although none of these drugs are considered antidepressants, their effects on depression were every bit as great as those of antidepressants."[193]

This finding increased Kirsch and Sapirstein's confusion. How is it that drugs that are not antidepressants are treating depression just as well as drugs that are? After some time, they came to at least one conclusion: The lowest common denominator of all these drugs is that they produce side effects. Kirsch explained the importance of this when he wrote,

> Why are side effects important? Imagine that you have been recruited for a clinical trial of antidepressant medication. As part of the required informed-consent procedure, you are told that you may be given a placebo instead of the active medication, but because this is a double-blind trial, you will not be told which you are getting until the study is over. You are told that it may take weeks before the therapeutic effects of the drug are apparent, and also that the drug has been reported to produce side effects in some patients. Furthermore, as required by the informed consent procedures that need to be followed in clinical trials, you are also told exactly what those side effects are (for example, a dry mouth, drowsiness, diarrhea, nausea, forgetfulness) and that these are most likely to occur soon after treatment has begun—before the therapeutic effects are felt. Now if I were a patient in one of these trials, I would wonder to which condition I had been assigned. Had I been put in the active-drug group or in the placebo group? Hmm, my mouth is getting dry, and I'm beginning to feel a little nauseous. Normally, I might feel distressed by these symptoms, but I have been informed that these are side effects of the active drug. So instead of feeling distressed, I am elated. My dry mouth and nauseous stomach tell me that I have been given the active drug, rather than the placebo. I'm starting to feel better already.[194]

Recall Kirsch's expertise in the placebo effect. His reflection here is not a loose set of thoughts that the side effects of antidepressants may have a tiny something to do with drug-versus-placebo response. On the contrary, his thoughts here are the opinions of a cutting-edge placebo researcher basing his judgment on decades of studying the placebo effect and an understanding of how that effect manifests itself in individuals subject to its power. Nevertheless, just how important could the placebo effect be in antidepressant efficacy?

When the statistics are completed, Kirsch argued, "The correlation between side effects and improvement when taking Prozac is .96, which is just about as high as a correlation can get."[195] For his readers that were not familiar with statistics, Kirsch emphasized, "It is exceptionally rare to find correlations this high in research. My colleague John Kihlstrom at the University of California at Berkeley calls data like this 'Faustian'—by which he means that researchers would sell their souls to obtain them."[196]

Furthermore, Kirsch was contacted by researchers in Italy who were not persuaded that side effects could be so important in the efficacy of antidepressants. So, with Kirsch, they used "their collection of all the published and unpublished clinical trials that GlaxoKlineSmith had conducted on their SSRI, Seroxat."[197] "The results of that analysis showed that once you adjust for drug-placebo differences in side-effects, differences in rates of improvement are no longer statistically significant."[198] Side effects play a powerful role in the efficacy of antidepressants, and it is likely they do so because of the placebo effect.

Over and beyond the relatively small difference between drug and placebo that was apparent in this meta-analysis, Kirsch argued that the tiny difference that did exist between drug and placebo might be caused by an "enhanced placebo effect," which itself was caused by side effects and "breaking blind" in clinical trials.[199] To see how important this can be, Kirsch pointed to active placebos. Active placebos—placebos that cause side effects—have been used in some clinical trials to determine whether side effects are causing an enhanced placebo effect. The vast majority of these trials do not find a clinically significant difference between the active placebo and the antidepressant drug.[200] These pieces of evidence support the conclusion that a placebo effect and a side-effect-enhanced placebo effect are responsible for the clear majority of the improvement experienced by patients receiving antidepressants. This evidence contradicts the chemical imbalance hypothesis.

Even if the results of Kirsch and Sapirstein's meta-analysis were thought to be compelling, good science requires replication. Considering the comments made on their first meta-analysis,[201] Kirsch performed another meta-analysis with a "more complete data set."[202] This time around, Kirsch and his colleagues used the United States Freedom of Information Act to obtain unpublished antidepressant trials. This was a crucial step to getting a more comprehensive look at the efficacy of antidepressants.[203]

It was a crucial step because a significant amount of the data on antidepressants had not been published. Companies who sponsor clinical trials do not have to publish the information about those trials to the public. Because drug companies mostly sponsor the trials, and drug companies are interested in making a profit, it is understandable that they are not eager to publish trials, which do not demonstrate a significant difference between their antidepressant medication and placebo. Kirsch thoroughly documents this publication bias.[204] He also referred to other studies, such as Melander, Ahlqvist-Rastad, Meijer, and Beermann, who argued that "for anyone who relies on published data alone to choose a specific drug, our result should be a cause for concern. Without access to all studies (positive as well as negative, published as well as unpublished) . . . any attempt to recommend a specific drug is likely to be based on biased evidence."[205]

However, and fortunately, the U.S. Food and Drug Administration (FDA) requires companies seeking approval for antidepressant medications to submit information on all trials that they have conducted on that medication "whether or not those trials have been published."[206] The Freedom of Information Act requires that the FDA share that information after being given an appropriate request. So, Kirsch's use of the Freedom of Information Act granted him access to all the clinical trials on FDA-approved antidepressants, whether or not those trials had been published, and the trials would all be of an FDA-approved quality.[207] Kirsch and colleagues gathered "the medical and statistical reviews of every placebo-controlled clinical trial for the treatment of depression by . . . Prozac, Paxil, Zoloft, Effexor, Serzone, and Celexa" that was submitted to the FDA.[208] Then he and his colleagues crunched the numbers.

In the meta-analysis using the information obtained by the Freedom of Information Act, Kirsch et al. found that nearly 80% of the "drug response was duplicated in the placebo groups."[209] This 20% difference between the drug and placebo translated into roughly 2 points on the Hamilton Depression Rating Scale (HAM-D; the scale used to measure depression and improvement in each study in this meta-analysis). However, a difference of 2 points on the HAM-D, although (barely) enough to be considered statistically significant, does not meet the threshold for clinical significance.[210] In short, the difference between drug and placebo is minuscule and virtually undetectable. And, of course, the difference between drug and placebo would still need to take into account Kirsch's previous findings on the power of side effects to produce an enhanced placebo effect.

After publishing his first meta-analysis in 1998, Kirsch's critics were primarily concerned with his data set and the analysis of it. However, "this time there were no doubts about the accuracy of our analysis. . . . As one defender of antidepressants phrased it . . . it is clear that antidepressants have relatively small, specific effects for patients who participate in the randomized clinical trials conducted by the pharmaceutical industry."[211] Kirsch's findings regarding the small difference between drug and placebo effects have been, with minute differences, replicated multiple times.[212]

Even an FDA-sponsored meta-analysis of the data by Khin, Chen, Yang, Yang, and Laughren found data that was "remarkably consistent"[213] with Kirsch's.[214] Thus, the data emphatically suggests that increasing neurotransmitters has a small, clinically insignificant effect on depression.

Concluding Thoughts and Discussion

The historical argument that depression is caused by a chemical imbalance was rooted in two complementary strands of argument. Drugs that decreased neurotransmitter levels seemed to induce depression. Drugs that increased neurotransmitter levels seemed to alleviate depression. However, a more precise, methodologically rigorous investigation of these two assumptions seems to clearly show that neither of these strands of argument carry much weight. Drugs that decrease neurotransmitter levels do not induce depression, and some perform as well as antidepressant drugs in treating depression. Drugs that increase neurotransmitter levels do not, in a clinically significant manner, treat depression better than placebo. And it is decidedly likely that the small statistical difference between antidepressant drugs, placebo, and treatment results is caused by an enhanced placebo effect related to side effects. The data reviewed in the preceding text has been replicated many times. In fact, Kirsch argued that "not only is the chemical-imbalance hypothesis unproven, but . . . it is about as close as a theory gets in science to being disproven by the evidence."[215] But if the evidence against the chemical imbalance hypothesis is so strong, why does it persist? There are at least four reasons.

The first reason is that powerful financial interests are invested in the billions of dollars in sales of antidepressants annually.[216] These financial interests, mostly pharmaceutical companies, spend millions of dollars advertising their antidepressants and courting doctors and psychiatrists.[217] Anyone who watches TV commercials regularly will have seen many advertisements for antidepressants; some have even included an animated demonstration of the chemical imbalance hypothesis.[218] So, it doesn't seem likely that these companies would be prone to pack up their tent and leave the market just because the data do not fit the story. If these companies believe they can continue to make profits and can continue to develop drugs that meet the FDA's approval guidelines, they will keep selling.

But isn't something off here? Didn't Kirsch obtain his data from the FDA? So, doesn't the FDA know that antidepressants don't perform, in a clinically significant way, better than placebos? And if so, why does the FDA continue to approve these drugs for public sale? As Kirsch has noted:

> The real answer to this question lies in the criteria that are used for antidepressant drug approval. The efficacy criterion used by drug regulators requires two "adequate and well-controlled" clinical trials showing that a drug is better than a placebo. But there are

some catches. The first catch is that there is no limit to the number of studies that can be run to find the two showing a statistically significant effect. Negative trials just don't count. The second catch is that the size of the drug–placebo difference—its clinical significance—is not considered.[219]

To illustrate this, consider the case of the SSRI antidepressant citalopram (marketed as Celexa). Seven clinical trials of this drug were submitted to the FDA during the approval process. Only two of them met the approval criteria—the others didn't show a significant difference between drug and placebo.[220] In effect, five of the seven studies were swept under the FDA's rug. And, as mentioned earlier, the FDA only requires antidepressant drugs to perform, in a *statistically significant* way, better than placebos. The FDA does not require antidepressant drugs to perform, in a *clinically significant* way, better than placebos.

This leads to the second reason that the chemical imbalance hypothesis thrives: Customers keep buying the product. Companies wouldn't sell antidepressants if there wasn't consumer demand. But why do the customers keep buying if the data shows that drugs are not better than placebos? First, many consumers are unaware of the research reviewed above. Second, many consumers taking antidepressants do feel better. On average, about 10 points on a HAM-D.[221] As demonstrated earlier, patients given placebos also feel about that much better. However, customers do not participate in a randomized control trial when they are prescribed antidepressants. A typical individual taking antidepressants prescribed by their doctor does not have a control version of themselves to compare their results with. All they experience is that they take an antidepressant and it makes them feel better. To them, drug effect and placebo effect are indistinguishable.

A third reason is that psychiatry, as a profession and practice, has a vested interested in maintaining that mental illnesses are genuinely biological illnesses, which are appropriately treated with psychotropic medication.[222] If it is the case that depression is not a chemical imbalance but, rather, a cognitive or social problem that manifests itself in the subjective experience of a person, then it could be that psychiatrists would serve most of their patients better by providing them with psychotherapy instead of prescribing drugs, especially long-term use, with a plethora of negative side effects.[223]

Fourth, much of academic research is strongly rooted in a philosophy of materialism and a related understanding of science. Many philosophers and scientists are skeptical of the notion that there is a disembodied soul or spirit lurking within our bodies. And even if there was such a soul, it wouldn't have a place in scientific methodology. So, it is common to think that a human mind is just his brain. "So," an academic researcher might ask, "if depression is not caused by a chemical imbalance then what is it caused by, evil spirits?" I am sympathetic to this joking question. I don't think there is a disembodied soul or spirit. Yet I also don't think that a mind is the same as a brain. And this—an applicable philosophy of mind—is the critical frontier for psychiatry and psychology. Fortunately, more work on this intersection between philosophy, science, brain, mind, psychiatry, and psychology is underway and I discuss this in more detail in Chapter Eight.

Chapter Five
Depression and Feminism

The diagnostic category of major depressive disorder includes a heterogeneous cluster of phenomenological states and behaviors, typified by experiences such as: sadness, lack of energy, lack of pleasure, hopelessness, weight changes, sleep difficulties, and psychomotor agitation/retardation.[224] Epidemiological data has identified that women meet the diagnostic criteria for depression at a rate of approximately 2:1 when compared with men;[225] this rate holds steady in medical populations.[226] Women are also prescribed selective serotonin reuptake inhibitors (SSRIs) at twice the rate of men.[227]

The conventional wisdom of mental health researchers and clinicians is that depression is best understood as a biopsychosocial (BPS) phenomenon with a variety of causes ranging from genetic to biochemical, environmental, and psychological.[228] Yet underneath the eclectic approach to depression inherent in the BPS model, a body of theoretical and scientific literature has attempted to refine our understanding of depression. These perspectives range from the validity of the concept of depression,[229] to its causes,[230] prevalence,[231] and available interventions.[232] Recently, there has been increased criticism of the BPS model of depression and, in turn, a renewed interest in biologically reductive explanations.[233] The underlying assumption of these more biologically-oriented views appears to be that since the brain underpins mental experience, brain abnormalities and/or neurochemical defects underpin depression.[234]

One of the most prominent examples of a biologically reductive explanation of depression is the chemical imbalance theory.[235] This theory has been enormously influential in both the academic and lay public populations.[236] However, there is little evidence supporting the chemical imbalance theory. Furthermore, explaining depression as due to chemical imbalances unrelated to one's environmental and social context marginalizes other contributing causes such as oppression, poverty, and psychological factors.

In contrast to the chemical imbalance hypothesis, many feminist theorists place intra-individual components at the center of depression, arguing that depression may be equated with oppression.[237] Feminist writings do not view depression as emerging from within a person but rather as a reaction to an oppressive society and environment that contribute to internal conflict and despair. This perspective began to develop as a distinct theoretical framework in the 1970s, when feminists began protesting the perceived gender bias in psychological and psychiatric formulations.[238] A feminist understanding of distress considers the perspective of the marginalized individual who experiences the phenomenon in question as quintessential.[239] Further, the focus is not only on stressful events but also the structural differences that influence women's experiences.[240] It challenges the current dominant approach, which is thought to disempower women by medicalizing and pathologizing their bodies and life experiences[241] while simultaneously diminishing or ignoring the political, social, and developmental inequalities that contribute to a woman's psychological state.[242]

Biologically reductive explanations of emotional distress, such as the chemical imbalance theory, are not benign. Consider the diminishing or ignoring of political, social, and development inequalities that contribute to women's depression. For instance, women experience more sexual abuse, rape, and domestic violence than men, and yet they are often ignored or said to be seeking attention rather than suffering the effects of trauma and oppression. For example, Hankin and Abramson acknowledge that sexual abuse is a common risk factor for mental distress, and yet they assert that a "depressogenic inferential style" interacts with abuse to cause a state of depression.[243] This study seems to suggest that it is not that experiencing sexual abuse is depressing but rather that there is something wrong with the way the woman inferred her experience that leads her to have emotional distress. Further, women are also blamed more often for the abuse of their children even though men are often the perpetrators in the context of domestic abuse.[244] Interestingly, "battered women's syndrome" sounds like the concept of major depressive disorder, yet only one is included in the official diagnostic manual. Rather than acknowledge the social and environmental circumstances that led a woman to become distressed, she is told, often, that her depression was caused by a chemical imbalance.

Feminist-inspired theorists have long argued that the mental health profession has played a key role in regulating the marginalized (i.e., women)[245] and reinforcing white male control.[246] One way in which members of the profession accomplish this is by using diagnostic constructs which imply that psychological problems originate within the individual, stemming from inherent predispositional factors (i.e., a chemical imbalance) and a lack of skills. The chemical imbalance theory serves to maintain the status quo, while feminist-inspired theories suggest evaluating social problems that lead women to become distressed.

As would be expected, a feminist-inspired view of distress also lends itself to alternative treatment approaches. The focus of intervention within a feminist framework is one that seeks to alter and/or reduce the effects of external factors that contributed to the woman's distress rather than trying to get the woman to adapt to an oppressive society.[247] Additionally, many feminist writers and therapists insist that women not be evaluated and categorized according to a male standard.[248] Rather, women are unique in their expression of distress and their experiences of oppression and adversity, and services designed to assist women in despair must consider and appreciate such differences if advances in care are ever to be made. Although it is beyond the scope of this chapter to give justice to the breadth of theoretical and empirical research within the domain of feminist frameworks of depression, the key aspects (i.e., women's empowerment, acknowledgment of societal and interpersonal contextual factors, changing the environment to increase life satisfaction, and challenging the status quo) are offered here as one alternative to the dominant bio-reductive models. Furthermore, it can be seen through this exemplification that how one conceptualizes emotional pain leads to drastically different treatment approaches and clinical interactions. In addition, it may profoundly affect how a woman comes to understand her sense of self.

Concluding Thoughts and Discussion

It is difficult to estimate the psychological impact on the women who are told their depression is caused by a chemical imbalance. Of course, women are not the only group to suffer, nor the only group to be told their depressing and oppressive experiences in life are irrelevant to their emotional distress. Nonetheless, women are significantly affected by the promotion of unfounded theories and treatment approaches for depression. The chemical imbalance theory suggests that women suffering depressive symptoms do not need to examine their social situation, their relationships, and the expectations and norms they operate within. Instead, this theory leads medical professionals to tell women that the primary or only reason they are experiencing depressive symptoms is because they have a biological pathology. It is hard to doubt that this narrative can contribute to the diminishment of women examining their situations and can undermine the power of women, in personal situations or in public, to challenge features and institutions which hamper their well-being.

Recent research supports this view. Studies have consistently found that individuals who endorse biological etiologies of psychological disorders have increased prognostic pessimism.[249] This means that individuals who conceive of their depression as solely or predominantly caused by biological factors—such as a chemical imbalance—expect to make less improvement. The primary mechanism of action behind this phenomenon is thought to be that individuals who more strongly believe in biological etiologies also more strongly believe in essentialist views of themselves in which their emotional and psychological experiences are thought to be entirely or largely outside of their influence or control.[250] This is important because one of the largest contributors to client improvement in treatment is client expectancy.[251] Put briefly, clients who expect improvement improve more. Thus, theories and explanations that are related to prognostic pessimism can be expected to diminish improvement.

The focus of intervention within a feminist framework is one that seeks to alter and/or reduce the effects of external factors that initially contributed to the woman's distress rather than suggesting women adapt to an oppressive society.[252] The central tenet of feminist therapy is to increase empowerment and assertiveness in women.[253] This is in direct conflict with medicalized understandings and treatment approaches, which have a disempowering effect on women and take for granted her social situation.[254] In other words, biologically reductive approaches based on the disproven theory of chemical imbalances subverts therapies focused on empowerment and change.

Despite their popularity, biologically reductive models of depression contradict the scientific evidence, often have negative clinical impacts, and undercut the importance of identifying and challenging oppressive social structures and norms which contribute to emotional distress. Feminist approaches to depression are one option for an alternative. Clients and practitioners may benefit from dissemination of the latest research findings, even if it challenges their existing explanatory frameworks.

Chapter Six
Explaining Depression in Clinical Settings

Recent research has identified potential clinical impacts resulting from both client and clinician etiological beliefs surrounding psychological disorders. This body of research has identified that etiological beliefs can influence clinician and client treatment preferences and outcome. Thus, there is reason to explore etiological beliefs, typically explanatory analogies, frequently used in clinical settings. This article discusses two common analogies of depression, including a description of these analogies, their prevalence, and their limitations. It then connects this discussion with potential clinical impacts.

The Chemical Imbalance and the Diabetes Analogies of Depression

In clinical settings, two prominent examples of analogies of depression are the chemical imbalance analogy and the diabetes analogy. A description of these analogies and the evidence related to them are presented. The conceptual and empirical considerations discussed suggest these analogies are not supported by the evidence and are misleading.

The chemical imbalance analogy of depression suggests that a deficiency in one or more neurotransmitters causes or contributes to depression. However, despite the shortcomings of this explanation of depression which were reviewed in the last chapter, evidence suggests that this explanation is frequently provided to patients seeking care.

Pies argued a chemical imbalance analogy was used in clinical practice when explaining the causes of depression to patients.[255] Davies, a psychiatrist, illustrated this when he described the type of analogy he often provided his clients:

> I'll often say something like the way Zoloft works, is, it increases the level of serotonin in your brain, and, presumably, the reason you're depressed or anxious is that you have some sort of a deficiency. And I say that not because I really believe it, because I know the

evidence really isn't there for us to understand the mechanism—I think I say that because patients want to know something. And they want to know that we as physicians have some basic understanding of what we're doing when we're prescribing medications.[256]

Just how common such analogies were/are in clinical practice is not known because, as far as I know, no studies have formally investigated the subject. Nevertheless, there is evidence that patients, and the public in general, generally believe that a chemical imbalance is a cause of depression. In 2006, nearly 80% of Americans agreed with the statement that a chemical imbalance in the brain is a cause of depression.[257] More recent studies have also found widespread endorsement of a chemical imbalance analogy of depression. For instance, Read, Cartwright, Gibson, Shiels, and Magliano identified that just under 67% of survey respondents identified a chemical imbalance as a cause of depression[258]—more than any other cause, including family stress, work stress, genes, or relationship problems.

In addition, qualitative studies have also demonstrated that the chemical imbalance analogy is communicated in clinical practice.[259] For instance, Buchman, Borgelt, Whiteley, and Illes documented a participant's description of his doctor's explanation of the need for medication: "Listen, you're never going to feel normal…you have a brain imbalance…you're going to go up and down for the rest of your life unless you correct it with medication."[260]

Some have argued that a clinician-expounded chemical imbalance analogy of depression is not widespread. Pies argued that a chemical imbalance analogy of depression was never "seriously propounded by well-informed psychiatrists" and that over-enthusiastic opponents of medication ignore the nuances of psychiatrists' claims.[261] Of course, Pies's claims avoid including all medical doctors who, as the qualitative evidence cited above indicates, frequently use this analogy. Regardless, Lacasse and Leo identified many instances of psychiatrists suggesting a chemical imbalance analogy of depression and these psychiatrists included multiple American Psychiatric Association (APA) presidents as well as informative depression leaflets from the APA.[262] At the least, psychiatrists have generally not challenged the analogy.[263] In sum, the chemical imbalance analogy, though dubious, is widely believed and, though exact figures are uncertain, likely to be frequently used in clinical practice.

Despite the evidence that physicians have communicated a chemical imbalance analogy in clinical practice, it should be noted that they are not the only, or perhaps even the primary, exponents of this hypothesis. Deacon and Baird discussed how the chemical imbalance analogy of depression was likely importantly influenced by direct-to-consumer advertising—and these advertisements increased patient requests for and physician prescribing of antidepressants.[264] This fact, however, arguably strengthens the importance of physicians providing accurate information, if only to address well-identified inaccurate beliefs held by their clients.

Like the chemical imbalance analogy of depression, an analogy between depression and diabetes is also frequently communicated in a healthcare setting as an explanation of depression. This analogy implies that depression is a disease, like diabetes, that it may be a chronic condition requiring lifelong management, and that those with depression should consume the appropriate medication in the same way that an individual with diabetes would administer insulin treatment.

Unlike the chemical imbalance analogy, which has been thoroughly criticized elsewhere, very few publications address the shortcomings of this analogy. Even the literature that has challenged the analogy[265] does not identify crucial limitations of the comparison. As a result, four central reasons that the depression-diabetes analogy is inaccurate are reviewed below.

First, unlike diabetes, there are no clinically actionable diagnostic biomarkers for depression. Although symptoms can often be an important precursor to being tested for diabetes, to be diagnosed with diabetes an individual must have their glucose levels measured through objective tests such as the A1C or FPG.[266] Compare this process to the diagnostic process for major depressive disorder (depression). Symptoms are not simply a precursor for diagnosis of depression, they are the final arbiter because "...even though there have been thousands of studies looking for biological markers of mental health problems such as depression or schizophrenia, none has proven clinically actionable. And, in truth, little has been replicable even in a research setting."[267] This statement from Thomas Insel is congruent with the position of the fifth edition of the Diagnostic and Statistical Manual (DSM-5), which asserts that there are no laboratory tests or biomarkers for depression,[268] a situation that continues to the present.[269]

Second, unlike diabetes, depression is not a discrete entity. Historically, understanding diseases as discrete entities was substantiated by the identification of various causal contributors. For instance, the discovery of treponema pallidum, the bacteria which causes syphilis, provided convincing evidence to conceptualize syphilis as a discrete entity *caused* by a particular, identifiable pathogen.[270] Similarly, although the causes vary, an essential component of diabetes is insulin irregularities.[271] In the case of both diseases, the presence of established and measurable biological contributors to the illness are central to understanding the disease as a discrete entity.

However, as discussed, there are no biological markers for depression. This points to an even deeper challenge: Depression itself is not a discrete concept. A diagnosis of depression is given after a clinical assessment which involves an interview with a health professional and, often, measurement via a depression screening tool such as the Beck Depression Inventory[272] or the Hamilton Rating Scale for Depression.[273] In order to meet the diagnostic criteria for depression, one must manifest five or more symptoms, during the same two-week period, that correspond to a list of symptoms contained in the DSM-5.[274] However, as long as the minimum criteria are met, a diagnosis of depression can be given. This means that the way depression presents itself to health professionals varies greatly. For instance, by presenting with different symptoms, an individual can meet the diagnostic criteria for depression in 227 diverse ways.[275] While many of these possibilities will rarely present in clinical or research contexts, recent research indicated that more than 170 different symptom combinations led to a diagnosis of depression.[276] Additionally, opposite symptoms satisfy the diagnostic criteria. For instance, both significant weight gain *or* significant weight loss, as well as insomnia *or* hypersomnia, are symptoms of depression.[277]

The heterogeneity of depression is also evident in screening assessments such as the BDI or HDRS. These assessments query for symptoms and their severity, then translate these into a sum-score which is meant to measure a singular underlying disorder. However, evidence suggests that these rating instruments do *not* measure a singular underlying disorder because they do not exhibit unidimensionality.[278] For an assessment instrument to exhibit unidimensionality, all the symptoms being measured should be strongly linked to a single primary factor. If the symptoms measured are strongly linked to several factors, then the instrument is multifactorial. Analysis has suggested that within the BDI and HRSD, between one and seven various factors have been identified and that occasionally these factors are not correlated.[279] This is powerful evidence that depression is not a discrete entity.

Third, unlike diabetes, depression can be successfully treated with psychotherapy. Although there are many ways in which psychotherapy and skills training can be useful for individuals diagnosed with diabetes—for instance, helping individuals maintain a healthy diet, helping individuals to use insulin treatment to optimum effect, or in managing the emotional distress related to their diabetes—it is understood that psychotherapy proper has no effect on the management of blood sugar levels.[280] The reason is unsurprising: Since diabetes is a form of insulin deficiency disorder and since there is no known way of psychotherapy to directly influence insulin levels, psychotherapy is not suitable treatment for diabetes. On the other hand, depression can be effectively treated with psychotherapy. For instance, numerous theoretical models of depression hypothesize that depression is a cluster of maladaptive beliefs which can be identified and modified via psychotherapeutic interventions.[281] Regardless of the psychotherapeutic interventions used, psychotherapeutic interventions are effective at treating depression.[282]

Fourth, unlike diabetes, depression responds to placebo treatment. The placebo effect in drugs designed to treat glucose levels is negligible.[283] On the other hand, the placebo effect in drugs designed to treat depression is large. As mentioned in discussion on chemical imbalances in Chapter Four, numerous meta-analyses have documented that there is only a small difference in clinical improvement when comparing antidepressants to placebo. This small difference is likely the result of non-drug factors, such as an enhanced placebo effect caused by side-effects,[284] and, regardless, the difference between drug and placebo is so small that it is clinically insignificant.[285]

Prevalence of the Diabetes Analogy

Just how prevalent is the depression-diabetes analogy in medical practice? Like estimating the prevalence of the chemical imbalance analogy in medical practice, as far as I know, there are no studies which directly investigate this. Still, there are numerous qualitative studies which suggest that it is common.[286] For instance, consider the following transcript segment of a participant describing her experience with her doctor: "One doctor....said this to me once, 'If you're a diabetic, would you stop taking your medication because you felt good?' And I said 'No.' Then she said, 'Well, why would you....stop taking the [antidepressant] medication because you feel good?'"[287] A similar idea was commonly found in Gibson, Cartwright, and Read.[288] For instance, when asked about depression and antidepressant medication, participants frequently made claims such as, depression is, "just like diabetes—a chemical shortage...I need serotonin uptake inhibitors—simple!" and, "My GP said that if I had diabetes I would need to take insulin forever, so not to worry that I appear to need to continue to take anti-depressants forever."[289]

In addition to medical practice, the depression-diabetes analogy can be found elsewhere. For instance, Angermeyer, Holzinger, Carta, and Schomerus identified that the National Alliance on Mental Illness (NAMI), a prominent mental health advocacy group, has suggested that psychological disorders, such as depression, are biological, medical illnesses like "cancer or diabetes."[290] Further, Hansell et al.,[291] found that NAMI's website presented dramatically biased information about depression which over-emphasized biological components of the disorder. Hansell et al. suggested that this bias may be related to the significant funding NAMI receives from pharmaceutical companies.[292] Regardless, there are a variety of information sources which provide explanations via a depression-diabetes analogy that are inaccurate which, in turn, suggest the importance of physicians recognizing the shortcomings of the analogy and avoiding its use.

Discussion

The two explanatory analogies reviewed above communicate an etiology of depression that fits nicely within a biological model. In fact, it is because of the relative simplicity of the biological model of illness that the analogies were attractive—they offered an easy-to-understand explanation of the client's presenting problems. However, this approach to psychological disorders raises at least three areas of concern.

First, these analogies are not supported by the evidence. This was discussed in detail previously. In sum, however, consider Insel's remarks that there are no clinically actionable biomarkers for psychological disorders.[293][294] This lack of evidential support means that the use of these analogies in clinical practice, without appropriate identification of their inaccuracies and shortcomings, appears to ignore the principle of informed consent, as well as a number of the American Medical Association's (AMA) ethical principles, such as being honest and maintaining accurate, up-to-date scientific knowledge which can be made available to patients.[295]

The second area of concern is that this approach to psychological disorders encourages the use of psychotropic drugs which generally have significant negative side effects and generally do not yield superior clinical outcomes. Many studies have identified that the more individuals endorse a biological model of psychological disorders the more likely they see medication as the preferred treatment.[296] At first glance, these findings are unsurprising: If an individual believes that their condition is caused by an underlying biological pathology, it is natural to infer that the appropriate treatment method is to target the biological pathology via the appropriate biological means (i.e., an antidepressant).

Although not everyone who uses antidepressants experience negative effects, many problems associated with antidepressants are thoroughly documented.[297] These effects range from small inconvenience (e.g., dry mouth) to life threatening (e.g., possible increased suicidal behavior in children and adolescents). In between these extremes are a wide variety of other negative effects, such as disturbing homeostasis in the brain and gut, greater risk of relapse upon discontinuation, increased apoptosis, disruption of attentional processes, increased levels of gastrointestinal dysfunction, abnormal bleeding, impaired sexual functioning, weight gain, hepatoxicity and hypersensitivity reactions, cardiovascular problems, osteoporosis and fractures, sleep disturbance, and hyperprolactinemia.[298] Alarmingly, some adverse effects, such as treatment emergent affective switches, obesity, and bleeding problems may persist even after discontinuing antidepressant treatment.[299] Compounding these problems is the relative lack of data surrounding adverse effects outside of clinical study reports. This is troublesome because clinical study reports are likely to underestimate adverse reactions and they provide no information about long term consequences.[300]

In response to the negative side effects of antidepressants, Andrews et al. argued, "The weight of current evidence suggests that, in general, antidepressants are neither safe nor effective, they appear to do more harm than good."[301] Carvalho et al. presented a milder conclusion while still strongly suggesting that psychotherapy be considered before antidepressant treatment. They wrote, "The findings of this review suggest that long-term treatment with new generation ADs should be avoided if alternative treatments are available."[302]

On the other hand, psychotherapy is generally as effective as antidepressant medication while avoiding almost all of the side effects associated with them. Numerous meta-analyses have found that psychotherapy and antidepressant medication yield similar clinical improvement.[303] For instance, Gartlehner et al. conducted a rigorous meta-analysis, which included 44 clinical trials, with the goal of comparing the benefits and harms of antidepressant and psychological therapies. They concluded that antidepressants and cognitive-behavioral therapy cause similar positive treatment outcomes for adult outpatients with mild to severe depression. Garlehner et al. also identified that treatment discontinuation because of side effects were "more than twice as high" for individuals receiving antidepressants compared to those receiving psychotherapy.[304] Similarly, De Matt et al. found that psychotherapy and antidepressant treatment produced no difference in clinical effectiveness at treatment termination but that participants taking antidepressants were twice as likely to relapse after treatment termination compared to those who participated in psychotherapy.[305] Along similar lines, Khan et al.[306] compared the outcomes of blinded versus un-blinded raters in studies examining comparative efficacy between antidepressants and psychotherapy. In addition to finding no difference between antidepressant treatment and psychotherapy, Khan et al. found that there was no significant difference between combined therapy (antidepressant plus psychotherapy) and psychotherapy alone. In sum, the above meta-analyses suggest that psychotherapy is as effective as antidepressant medication in treating depression. Importantly, they find that psychotherapy avoids most of the side effects, as well as the higher discontinuation and remission rates, of antidepressant treatment. Thus, there is strong reason to believe psychotherapy should be considered just as viable, if not more viable, as antidepressants as a front-line treatment for individuals who experience depression—a treatment guideline that is pushed to the margins by analogies like the chemical imbalance and depression-diabetes analogies.

Alternative Etiologies

For the reasons discussed above, there are numerous reasons for professionals discussing depression with clients to avoid analogies such as the chemical imbalance and depression-diabetes analogies. In their place, recent research suggests that alternative forms of explanation are not only more congruent with the scientific evidence but can also contribute to positive treatment outcomes. For example, Lebowitz and Ahn conducted a study in which participants in the intervention condition were presented with a seven-minute psychoeducational video emphasizing the malleability of biological factors involved in depression.[307] This video emphasized the importance of epigenetics and how biology can be altered via experience—such as psychotherapy. The control condition was not presented with the psychoeducational video. Both conditions completed a variety of assessments designed to measure etiological beliefs, prognosis, etc. Results of the study indicated that participants in the intervention condition significantly decreased prognostic pessimism related to depression and that this change was maintained six weeks post intervention. Although this area of research is new, similar effects of malleability psychoeducation have already been identified[308] and have been suggested as important to innovative mental health treatment.[309] This research suggests that alternative explanatory approaches more closely track the current state of scientific research surrounding the causes of depression; these approaches also appear to have significant clinical advantages.

Chapter Seven
Mental Disorders and Stigma

In early 2016, Lena Dunham, a well-known actress, received attention and praise because of a collection of Instagram photos she publicly posted. These photos highlighted her mental disorders and the medications she uses to decrease her distress. Her central message was that there should be "no shame" surrounding mental illnesses or the use of medications.[310] By "shame," Dunham appeared to be referring to the stigma surrounding mental illnesses, which is pervasive and has a variety of negative effects, such as increasing distress and discouraging individuals from seeking help.[311] Due to the widespread, negative effects of stigma, mental health patients, mental health advocacy organizations, mental health professionals, researchers, celebrities, and politicians have communicated their commitment to ending stigma through psychoeducational campaigns.

For example, actress Glenn Close co-founded an organization called Bring Change 2 Mind, and its purpose is to "end stigma and discrimination surrounding mental illness" through education. The method for combating stigma endorsed by Dunham and Close appears to rely on explaining mental illnesses as brain disorders. For instance, the "facts" section of the Bring Change 2 Mind website states that "the fact is, a mental illness is a disorder of the brain—your body's most important organ—and one in four adults experience mental illness in a given year, including depression, bipolar disorder, schizophrenia, and PTSD."[312]

By asserting that mental illnesses are brain disorders, this approach highlights supposed brain defects as causes of mental disorders. This, in turn, challenges the stigmatizing belief that mental disorders are the result of a moral failure or character weakness. The reasoning goes: You wouldn't blame someone for being diagnosed with a physical disease to which they did not contribute. So, why would you blame someone for their mental illness, since mental illnesses are really brain disorders to which they did not contribute?

This approach to stigma has been extensively studied. For example, Corrigan et al. summarized the perspective used by Dunham when they wrote, "Moral models yield attributions that mental illness is onset controllable and persons with mental illness are to blame for their symptoms. Biological models are more consistent with attributions that mental illness is uncontrollable at onset."[313] In other words, moral models suggest that individuals can control the development of their mental disorders while biological models suggest they cannot. This is in line with Bring Change 2 Mind's claim that "like most diseases of the body . . . mental illnesses are no one's fault."[314]

It seems to me that identifying and challenging stigma are excellent goals, and I praise individuals and groups, like those mentioned above, for their efforts. However, I am also concerned because I believe there are at least three important problems with this approach.

The first problem: The assertion that mental disorders are "brain disorders" contradicts the scientific data and some important philosophic considerations underlying those data. To begin, consider, again, what Thomas Insel, the head of the National Institute for Mental Health until November of 2015, wrote near the end of his tenure: "The problem is that even though there have been thousands of studies looking for biological markers of mental health problems such as depression or schizophrenia, none has proven clinically actionable. And, in truth, little has been replicable even in a research setting."[315] Insel's comments are not out of the ordinary. Congruent statements have been made by many mental health experts.[316] In sum, scientific research has not identified reliable biological pathologies causing mental disorders. And it is a plausible argument that if we've not identified biological pathologies, it is a stretch to call mental disorders "brain disorders" or "brain diseases."

Perhaps it is true that researchers may someday identify biological pathologies—or, as the RDoC suggests, disordered brain circuits. Even if they do not, at the least, it seems to me that mental illnesses still involve or are mediated by the brain.[317] And as neuroscience continues to progress, it is likely that more and more precise correlations between mental illnesses and brain structure and function will be discovered. But even these discoveries would not immediately justify understanding mental disorders as brain disorders, because a change in the brain is not synonymous with a brain disorder.

Let me explain: All mental phenomena and behaviors are mediated by the brain. That is, everything changes our brain, from our developmental environment to stressful life events, falling in love, studying for an exam, meditating, and participating in psychotherapy.[318] So, even if researchers reliably identified brain differences in individuals who experience, for example, chronic anxiety, this does not lead to the conclusion that a disordered brain is causing the anxiety. It merely identifies that the brain changes in response to experiences. To illustrate this point, consider a study in which researchers identified that when individuals diagnosed with social anxiety are administered cognitive-behavioral psychotherapy, their distressful symptoms diminished, *and* their brains changed.[319] Crucially, the mechanism involved in changing the brain was not primarily biological but psychological. Changing their unhelpful beliefs and behaviors significantly diminished their social anxiety and changed their brains.

An objection I have often heard to this sort of example is that even though the mechanism of change may be psychological, the change still occurs *fundamentally* at the biological level. This objection opens a larger discussion which I discuss in the Introduction. For now, I will try to briefly explain an important aspect of my reply to this type of reductionist objection.

If *fundamentality* is what we are after, then mental disorders are not really brain disorders but, instead, patterns of quarks (or quantum fields or whatever else physics identifies) interacting with each other ways. In fact, from this type of reductionist perspective, sciences such as chemistry and biology aren't real; they are useful fictions— epistemological tools with pragmatic explanatory powers that scientists use until our understanding of physics becomes powerful enough to achieve our explanatory goals. So, if we want to be scientific about mental disorders, then we need to rely not on neuroscientists, psychiatrists, psychologists, and those who have experienced mental illness, but on physicists.

I hope you will agree with me that this sort of thinking does not make much sense. It is important to note that many biologically oriented researchers agree that this perspective is not comprehensive or functional. For example, Kendler argued, "It is possible to study scientific questions from perspectives that are both too basic and too abstract,"[320] and this is why he thought it important to reject looking for "big, simple neuropathological explanations for psychiatric disorders"[321] and instead accept that in "ways we can observe but not yet fully understand, subjective, first-person mental phenomena have causal efficacy in the world."[322] In short, psychosocial factors are crucial to understanding the development of mental disorders and approaches which emphasize only biological features, such as claiming that mental disorders are brain disorders, overstate the current evidence and are deeply misguided.

Now that we have gotten muddy in that philosophical swamp, I want to return to the subject of combating stigma. My next concern is straight-forward: A significant body of evidence suggests that emphasizing biogenetic etiologies of mental disorders does not reduce stigma. For instance, Angermeyer et al. used a population-based study design to investigate "the question whether promulgating biogenetic explanations may help reduce the stigma attached to mental illness and, therefore, should be included into anti-stigma messages."[323] They found that biogenetic explanations are linked to increased stigmatizing attitudes and, as a result, should be avoided in anti-stigma campaigns.

Their findings are not unusual. In fact, they are the established finding in the field. Similar outcomes are found in numerous studies and meta-analyses.[324] Even recent experimental studies suggest that biogenetic etiologies of mental disorders increase perceived differentness—such as increased perceived incompetence and unpredictability—and do not reduce stigma or explanations that emphasize that mental disorders may not be discrete diseases.[325]

When I first examined this evidence, I was perplexed. If biogenetic etiologies emphasize that individuals are not responsible for their mental disorders—their genetics, brains, and/or chemical imbalances are—then why do biogenetic etiologies not decrease, but often increase, stigma? Well, in short, the research has identified that stigma is not only comprised of responsibility. For instance, Schomerus et al. emphasized that while biogenetic etiologies of mental disorders are often associated with reduced levels of perceived responsibility and blame, these reduced levels can be "outweighed by the adverse effects mediated by perceived differentness and dangerousness, respectively,"[326] and similar findings are common. These increased levels of perceived differentness and dangerousness can contribute to the negative effects of stigma that organizations like Bring Change 2 Mind are attempting to challenge. Thus, it seems to me that there is good reason to rethink this strategy.

So, given my concerns, where does this leave us? Unfortunately, there is no quick and easy solution. Corrigan et al. noted that "advocates need to learn from the complex research on stigma change to implement programs that improve care seeking while not exacerbating other forms of discrimination."[327] That is not easy, because mental disorders and stigma are large, often complicated subjects. It's important to recognize, though, that there are alternatives to biogenetic etiologies of mental disorders—such as psychosocial approaches—that are congruent with the scientific evidence and may avoid promoting stigmatizing attitudes. That is, individuals who experience mental disorders may be responding to harmful environments and/or lack the knowledge/resources to manage their lives in more adaptive ways. This perspective does not reduce mental disorders to brain disorders, and it does not imply that we should blame individuals for their mental illnesses. It seems to me that this is an approach worth considering.

Chapter Eight
Neuroessentialism

The biopsychosocial model is the conventional wisdom of today's mental health practitioners.[328] It is meant to integrate biological, psychological, and sociological factors into a comprehensive etiological narrative. But how these three distinct spheres interconnect is poorly understood. As a result, narrower accounts of psychological disorders continue to be developed and used. This chapter, divided into five sections, critically discusses one of these accounts in the etiological explanation of depression: neuroessentialism. Section One defines neuroessentialism and identifies its prevalence. Section Two discusses antecedents to neuroessentialism. Section Three reviews theoretical concerns surrounding neuroessentialism. Section Four reviews the empirical studies that substantiate those concerns. Section Five discusses some implications for mental health professionals. Neuroessentialistic conceptualizations of depression can have negative clinical impacts on individuals receiving mental health treatment. These impacts need to be considered by treatment providers.

Neuroessentialism

Neuroessentialism is the view that the definitive way of explaining human psychological experience is by reference to the brain and its activity from chemical, biological, and neuroscientific perspectives. The underlying assumption of neuroessentialism is that "for all intents and purposes, we are our brains"[329] and "mental processes are either identical with brain processes or exclusively realized by brain processes."[330] For instance, if someone is experiencing depression, a neuroessentialistic perspective would claim that he or she is experiencing depression because his or her brain is functioning in a certain way.

Neuroessentialistic conceptualizations are growing in prominence. Neuroessentialistic concepts are found in academic research and in the culture at large. Satel and Lilienfeld pointed out, "You've seen the headlines: This is your brain on love. Or God. Or envy. Or happiness. And they're reliably accompanied by articles boasting pictures of color-drenched brains."[331] The interest in the brain has become a part of many academic research programs in areas such as "neurolaw, neuroeconomics, neurophilosophy, neuromarketing, and neurofinance."[332] Frazzetto and Anker characterized this growing appeal and prominence of brain-based explanations as part of a widespread "rise of a neuroculture," which they argued "is hardly surprising as neuroscience carries promises of revealing the underpinnings of our [. . .] emotions, consciousness, the way we make decisions, and our sociopsychological interactions."[333]

In addition to combating stigma, at least two other factors appear to have nurtured neuroessentialistic thinking: the predominance of reductionism in psychiatry and the market for psychotropic medicine.

Reductionism in Psychiatry

The reductionist view in psychiatry is not new. Emil Kraepelin argued for some version of it at the beginning of the 20th century.[334] For instance, Kraepelin argued that many psychological disorders, such as schizophrenia, "are best understood as biological diseases"[335] and that psychological disorders "are the result of heredity, chemical imbalances, and metabolic irregularities."[336] Many psychiatrists have followed his lead.[337] Yet Kraepelin's influence and esteem varied over the 20th century, during which alternative psychological and social explanations of mental disorders were suggested.[338] However, the rise of neuroscience, especially new brain imaging techniques, has put reductive conceptualizations of psychological disorders back in the spotlight. Gruen argued, "Brain structures, genes, and neurotransmitters have been seen as directly determining depression . . . [u]nderstanding neural circuitry is being equated with understanding the experience of fear and depression."[339] Gold and Stoljar elaborated on this sort of conceptualization:

> Many scientists and philosophers adhere to the metaphysical view sometimes known as materialism. Roughly, materialism holds that psychological events, states, and processes are nothing more than events, states, and processes of the brain. Given these two views and treating neuroscience by definition as the science of the brain, it seems inevitable that the neuron doctrine is true: if the mind is the brain, and if neuroscience is the science of the brain, then it

is practically a fact of logic that neuroscience is the science of the mind, and that it alone will explain what can be explained about the mind.[340]

Over the past two decades, commitments to reductionism contributed to a significant increase in brain disease conceptualization of psychological disorders in neuroscientific and psychiatric research.[341] This significant increase has contributed to neuroscience's status as the "poster child" for medical sciences.[342] In the same way that behaviorism attempted to ground psychology in the methodology of the natural sciences, neuroessentialistic viewpoints attempt to ground psychological experience and disorders in the methodology of neuroscience.

Despite the widespread neuroessentialistic conceptualization of psychological disorders, however, the *Diagnostic and Statistical Manual of Mental Disorders, Fifth Edition* (DSM-5) preserved a place for the psychological in mental disorders. In the *DSM-5*, symptoms and client self-reports are still primary in diagnosis. According to the *DSM-5*, "there are no laboratory tests, x-rays, or other biological markers for any mental disorder; there is no physiological specificity to any mental disorder; there is no genetic specificity to any mental disorder."[343] However, as we discussed in previous chapters, the National Institute of Mental Health launched the Research Domain Criteria (RDoC) to replace the DSM with a new research program and classification scheme that is hoped to provide more valid and reliable diagnoses and, in turn, better treatment outcomes. According to the former director of the National Institute of Mental Health, the RDoC is needed because:

> Unlike our definitions of ischemic heart disease, lymphoma, or AIDS, the *DSM* diagnoses are based on a consensus about clusters of clinical symptoms, not any objective laboratory measure. In the rest of medicine, this would be equivalent to creating diagnostic systems based on the nature of chest pain or the quality of fever. Indeed, symptom-based diagnosis, once common in other areas of medicine, has been largely replaced in the past half century as we have understood that symptoms alone rarely indicate the best choice of treatment.[344]

Proponents of the RDoC argue that symptoms may be clinically useful but relying on them alone is primitive medicine.[345] Instead, the RDoC conceptualizes mental disorders as follows:

> (1) Mental disorders are presumed to be disorders of brain circuits. (2) Tools of neuroscience, including neuroimaging . . . can be used to identify dysfunctions of neural circuits. (3) Data from genetics research and clinical neuroscience will yield biosignatures that will augment . . . clinical intervention.[346]

Insel claimed that the "RDoC is nothing less than a plan to transform clinical practice by bringing a new generation of research to inform how we diagnose and treat mental disorders."[347] The RDoC has accepted as its working hypothesis that the cause of mental disorders is disordered brain circuitry and the proper approach to diagnosis and treatment is to identify what those circuits are and how to modify them for the best treatment outcomes. In other words, proponents of the RDoC claim that "all mental processes take place in brain tissue; therefore mental disorders must be brain disorders."[348]

Market for Medicine

Pharmaceutical drug use for a variety of mental disorders has sharply increased over the past several decades.[349] To illustrate this rise, consider the increased use of antidepressants. According to estimates from Pincus et al., from 1985 to 1994, the "proportion of psychiatric visits for depression that included a prescription of a psychopharmacological agent increased from 53.5% to 70.9%."[350] A similar increasing trend in the use of antidepressants was discussed by Olfson and Marcus, who identified that:

> Between 1996 and 2005, the overall annual rate of antidepressant treatment among persons 6 years and older increased from 5.84 to 10.12 per 100 persons. This corresponds to a national increase from 13.3 million persons in 1996 to 27 million persons in 2005.[351]

Antidepressant medications approved by the Food and Drug Administration are "blockbuster drugs," with about 10% of Americans over the age of 12 taking at least one.[352] Among women, the prevalence is higher. For example, almost one in four women (22%) within the ages of 40 and 59 takes antidepressant medication.[353]

There are numerous plausible explanations for this significant rise in the use of antidepressants. First, millions of individuals experience significant distress in their lives, which may be related to depression. Most want to reduce or eliminate this distress, especially if this can be achieved quickly and easily via medication. Medications are a quick, cheap, and convenient option. Second, there is evidence that the significant increase in direct-to-consumer (DTC) advertising for antidepressants is related to rising prescription rates.[354] Such advertisements portray depression as a biological medical condition that can successfully be treated with medicine.[355]

Park and Grow reviewed the literature on the effects of DTC advertising of antidepressants and suggested that at least two factors of DTC advertising are plausibly linked to increased antidepressant use: (1) an increase in the perceived prevalence of depression, which leads to higher perceived risk, and (2) brand promotion.[356] These two factors work together by suggesting to a large pool of potential consumers that they are at a higher risk for depression than they previously believed; that experiences they may often have—such as feeling fatigue, disinterest, sadness, or having trouble concentrating or sleeping—could be caused by depression; and that there are medications that effectively treat depression. Deacon pointed out that it is presently common for patients to request antidepressant medication from their mental health care providers, largely because of DTC advertising.[357] The result of these factors is increased use of antidepressants. As such, it is not entirely surprising that psychiatric medication sales are worth tens of billions of dollars annually—$70 billion in 2010.[358]

Theoretical Considerations

Neuroessentialism's rising prominence has attracted critics from a variety of perspectives. We will now review criticism from philosophic, humanistic, and neuroscientific perspectives.

Much of the philosophic criticism of neuroessentialism is rooted in debates within the philosophy of science and the philosophy of mind.[359] Some of these debates include questions such as the following: What is the relationship between reductionism and the special sciences, such as the relationship between physics on the one hand

and chemistry, biology, and psychology on the other? What counts as a scientific explanation? Are the concepts used in neuroscience coherent?

Recall the passage from Gold and Stoljar.[360] This passage pointed out that many scientists rely on a reductionist, materialistic ontology. Thus, from this perspective, it is almost a matter of definition that mental disorders are *really* brain disorders. Something like this appears to be what the proponents of the RDoC have in mind. However, Graham challenged the concern raised by Gold and Stoljar when he wrote,

> We should remind ourselves that, despite the unpopularity of dualism in mental health science, a distinction between mental and non-mental somatic or physical disorders is widely accepted within medicine. . . . Does it imply that the mental is something non-physical? No, it does not. . . . The world in which we live in is a hierarchically layered or multi-leveled world. . . . Physics describes the most basic or general level, chemistry a level above that, and biology, psychology, and sociology each describe successively higher and more abstract and specialized levels. . . .. We persons are special or distinct in our detailed multi-level complexity. . . . So to be us ultimately is to be physically based or realized. This does not mean, however, that each and every activity, state, aspect or component of us can be exhaustively or completely described in lower level physical scientific terms.[361]

Graham is presenting two related but distinct arguments. Graham's first argument is that special sciences, such as chemistry, biology, psychiatry, and clinical psychology, should not worry about ontological concerns related to reduction if they can produce reliable, predictive, and useful information.[362] For example, a cognitive theory of depression that hypothesizes that depression is often caused by particular types of beliefs can, at the same time, assume that beliefs are, in a complete theory of physics, nothing but subatomic particles arranged in a particular way—from quarks to molecules to neurons to a brain. However, since contemporary physics is not currently at this level of sophistication, scientists can make do with "cruder" cognitive theories until physics reaches an appropriate level of sophistication. In Graham's view, this is acceptable if the cognitive theories are proficient at reliably producing predictive, useful information.

Graham's second argument is that it is plausible that higher level phenomena, such as subjective experience and psychological disorders, may never be reducible to lower level scientific terms.[363] Thus, to understand depression, it is important to consider someone's brain, beliefs, and social context. For instance, the stock market crash of 2008 has been found to increase feelings of depression and use of antidepressants.[364] The explanation for these increases is unlikely to be a spontaneous, unpredictable spike in brain diseases. Instead, it is likely explained by individuals whose life circumstances have taken a turn for the worse via decreased wealth, unemployment, and other difficulties.[365]

Another illustration of Graham's argument[366] can be found in a study by Alva Noë: Imagine a group of scientists examining a dollar bill with the greatest technology available.[367] The dollar bill's subatomic structure has been carefully mapped with the best physics. Yet even the most comprehensive physics is not able to identify the market value of the dollar within the subatomic structure of the paper. Of course, the value of a dollar does not exist within the dollar but emerges in the context of a larger system. In other words, certain features of the world require an appeal to more abstract concepts to be explained, and this is true even if these more abstract concepts do not contradict those physical explanations. That is, physicists studying a dollar will not find particles that defy the laws of physics, but they also will not find the dollar's market value.

Another philosophical consideration centers on what counts as an explanation. Recall that neuroessentialism explains psychological disorders as disordered brains. However, Dretske suggested that various levels of explanation are involved in science and are required for a comprehensive account of psychological phenomena.[368] To illustrate this, he presented an example focused on a flower that changes color from red to white during the spring season. What *explains* the color change? One explanation will have to do with the chemical and biological structure of the flower and the color pigments that are caused by that structure. Yet an evolutionary biologist may not be content with that explanation. The evolutionary biologist might point out, for example, that in the spring, a type of beetle migrates into the flower's habitat, searching for flowers to consume. For one reason or another, this beetle is only attracted to red flowers, which the beetle then consumes. From an evolutionary perspective, the flower's color change is explained as random adaptation that has been selected because of its survival value. That is, when spring—and the beetles—come, the flower changes from red to white and, since the beetles are only attracted to red flowers, this color change protects the flower from the beetles' hungry attention.

What is apparent is that the explanation of the flower's color change varies based on the level of explanation. The explanation from an evolutionary biologist is much different, though not contradictory, from the explanation offered by molecular biologists or botanists. The explanation is different because the evolutionary biologist is focused on the system the flower is a part of (as well as the forces of evolution), while the molecular biologist is focused on the specific chemical and biological processes that make up the flower and are involved with its changing color. A similar line of thinking could apply to psychological disorders. For instance, an individual experiencing depression has a brain that functions in a certain manner. It is possible that sometime in the future neuroscientists can reliably identify forms of brain function or structure that are reliably correlated with depression. But even then, this would not be an exhaustive explanation of depression for the same reason that the flower's molecular structure is not an exhaustive explanation of color change. In fact, the evolutionary value of depressive symptoms has been discussed at length by numerous researchers and clinicians.[369]

A third philosophic criticism of neuroessentialism is that numerous neuroscientists have made conceptual mistakes that exaggerate the explanatory power of neuroscience. The neuroscientist-philosopher duo of Bennett and Hacker identified a pattern of neuroscientists asserting that the brain perceives, thinks, guesses, knows, etc. and that these functions are explained by the brain's neural activity.[370] These neuroscientists appear to believe that comprehensive identification of neural activity can replace psychological explanations. Bennett and Hacker agreed that maturing neuroscience will be able to identify a continually greater amount of the neural underpinnings of perceiving, thinking, and so on via inductive correlation between neural activity and psychological phenomenon. However, they argued that this process cannot replace psychological explanations because an explanation of a human being's perceiving, acting, or thinking cannot be accomplished by focusing on the brain alone.

Why?

Bennett and Hacker argued that focusing solely on the brain to explain, for example, thinking, is committing the mereological fallacy in which an attribute of a whole entity is mistakenly applied to a part.[371] To demonstrate this, consider how neuroscientists identify neural correlates. First, they must identify psychological concepts, such as thinking, believing, intending, and so on. Only after these concepts have been identified are neuroscientists in a position to examine the neural underpinnings involved in these psychological processes. So, for example, if a neuroscientist was identifying the neural activity associated with thoughts, such as "it's hopeless," he or she cannot include only the brain in his or her study. The neuroscientist must also rely on the report of the human being who possesses the thought. That is, to correlate the thought that it is hopeless with neural activity, the neuroscientist starts with the psychological phenomenon and then looks for neural manifestation. Subjective experience guides neural mapping, and the neural map is not the same thing as the subjective territory. Therefore, Bennett and Hacker argued that agreement on "what counts as a manifestation of consciousness is a precondition for scientific investigations into the neural conditions for being conscious. Otherwise one could not even identify what one wants to investigate."[372]

Humanistic Considerations

Humanistic psychologists have long argued against reductionist perspectives in psychology. Rogers was troubled by the methodology of many psychologists of his time. He wrote, "One of the great mistakes in the behavioral sciences today . . . is that since our science must deal in observables . . . we have assumed that the pattern we sense must also have to do with observables."[373]

The trouble with this way of thinking is that the object being studied—human experience and behavior—is reduced to the observable manifestations being measured. But a human being is not only his behavior—especially not only behavior in experimental settings. Human beings also possess "internal, ineffable, subjective, and invisible" aspects that, despite their lack of observability, powerfully influence human experience and behavior.[374]

Frankl, another preeminent thinker from a humanistic perspective, argued against reductionist thinking in psychology for decades.[375] For example, Frankl argued that "the human quality of a human being is disregarded and neglected, for example, by those psychologists who adhere to either *the machine model* or *the rat model*."[376] In Frankl's view, the problem with these models is that they attempt comprehensive explanations of human beings from a limited perspective, whether that perspective is biological, psychoanalytic, behaviorist, or any other. These limited perspectives are poorly equipped to integrate the human capabilities of self-detachment and self-transcendence. These capabilities allow human beings to be aware of themselves and their surroundings and to make free choices about their attitudes. Without integrating these capabilities, reductionist perspectives (machine model or rat model) describe only particular dimensions of human beings that will not be comprehensive or even most important.

Yet Frankl appeared to believe that such models, though often presented in a manner that exaggerated their explanatory power, had a place in psychology and psychiatry. He recalled that he was once asked in an interview "whether I as a professor of neurology and psychiatry would not concede that man is subject to conditions and determinants."[377] His reply was that he knew very well many of the conditions and determinants of human beings, but that he also knew very well their ability to detach and transcend from those conditions. Due to his belief in the ability of human beings to detach and transcend their situation, he suggested a dimensional ontology, which integrates multiple perspectives of human beings in a way that recognizes conditions, determinates, detachment, and transcendence. He illustrated this dimensional ontology by pointing out that a cylinder, when viewed exclusively from the top or the bottom, looks like a two-dimensional circle. Reductionists, Frankl argued, take the circle to be all there is because it is all their perspective enables them to observe. Yet only by incorporating other perspectives is a comprehensive understanding of the cylinder possible. The same is true of human beings—a point that is apropos considering the problem of fragmentation involved in the biopsychosocial model.[378]

Following this line of thinking, Frankl suggested that depression cannot be understood as a one-size-fits-all phenomenon.[379] Instead, Frankl proposed that depression could be understood as endogenic, psychogenic, sociogenic, and/or noogenic. Frankl was willing to entertain the possibility that some forms of psychological disorder had their etiological origins in heredity and biochemistry, while others were rooted in other factors, such as difficult life circumstances and/or underlying unresolved beliefs of life's meaninglessness. Regardless of etiology, Frankl claimed that assisting clients to find meaning in the struggles of their lives can largely diminish their suffering even if it cannot eliminate their troublesome circumstances. This is why Frankl wrote that it is often "overlooked or forgotten that if a person has found the meaning sought for, he is prepared to suffer, to offer sacrifices, even, if need be, to give his life for the sake of it."[380]

Subsequent humanistic psychologists were also strong critics of deterministic thinking.[381] For example, Smith argued that humanistic psychologists were not opposed to science but to a science that focused solely on the "positivistic dogmas."[382] A humanistic science, in contrast to a narrow reductionistic view, would consider not only objectively observable biomarkers and behavior but also comprehensive human embeddedness, subjectivity, meaning, agency, and self-reports. Garrison summarized this when he pointed out that humanistic psychologists emphasized the centrality of human capacities and values, such as "ethics, truth, beauty, wholeness, spontaneity, and creativity" and that attempting to comprehensively understand human experience without reference to these concepts is impossible.[383]

The impact that humanistic objections had on reductionist methodology is difficult to overstate. For example, consider the steep decline of behaviorism. Not only did humanistic considerations influence many psychologists to incorporate methodologies and information outside of the behaviorist prescriptions, but even prominent behaviorists were affected. For example, when psychologists with a strong empirical emphasis, like Bandura, embraced a more holistic view of human beings that incorporated participant self-reports into their experiments, this incorporation yielded predictive information over and beyond the information that could be obtained by strict behaviorist methodology.[384] In fact,

Bandura argued that a human being is not a "sack of potatoes" that can be understood through purely mechanistic forces.[385] Rather, human beings are agents who participate in creative, constructive purposes, and their awareness of themselves, their situations, and their beliefs makes a difference in their lives.

In sum, humanistic concerns about reductionism have made a significant impact on the psychological debate.[386] In fact, humanistic concerns have made an important impact on neuroscientific thinking, which will be discussed further on.[387]

Neuroscientific Considerations

Neuroscientists have also challenged neuroessentialism. Beauregard pointed out that "mainstream neuroscientists—scientists like me, who study the brain and how it works—operate from the view that electrical impulses in the brain account for all of our thought patterns and mental experiences."[388] This is, more or less, the neuroessentialistic perspective. However, Beauregard argued that evidence from a variety of directions—such as the power of placebo, hypnosis, and neurofeedback—"show us very different models of what is real and what is possible than materialist science permits. They also give us tools with which we can explore the nature of the relationship between our minds . . . and our brains."[389]

The writings of many other neuroscientists support Beauregard's view that numerous neuroscientists are suggesting conceptions of the mind that are at odds with neuroessentialism. For instance, Slaby and Gallagher argued that neuroessentialistic conceptions of the mind are at odds with evidence that shows the importance of the environment for mental processes.[390] Extended conceptions of the mind, sometimes called embodied cognition or situated cognition, are attracting the interest of numerous neuroscientists.

This view of the mind:

> [...] includes neural processes as [a] necessary but not sufficient component. This not only moves us beyond the . . . idea that cognition is something that happens . . . "in the head," but also towards a more enactive and intersubjective conception of mind.[391]

In their view, understanding phenomenological experience requires paying attention to neural processes as well as environmental structures and processes. These environmental structures and processes "couple"—form a reciprocal causal relationship—with phenomenological awareness and enable higher levels of cognitive performances.

A common, though simple, example of the extended mind in action is counting on one's fingers. In this case, the cognitive process of arithmetic, with its neural underpinnings, is coupled with an environmental place holder (the fingers), and the interaction between the cognitive/neural process and the fingers enables more efficient arithmetic. A more complicated example would be the process of writing an academic paper, in which thoughts mingle with notes, word processers, academic journals, Google scholar, and so on.[392] In both cases, the brain, the environment, and the mind are involved in dynamic, iterated loops in which each element is an important contributor to phenomenological experience and the neural processes involved in that experience. Wilson described this as off-loading cognitive work onto the environment. "The advantage is that by doing actual physical manipulation, rather than computing a solution in our heads, we save cognitive work."[393]

Clark described another example of the way in which contemporary neuroscience is integrating extended conceptions of mind.[394] After discussing a variety of bottom-up neural processes and top-down cognitive processes that influence those neural processes, Clark concretized this discussion by referencing ongoing work in mobile robotics. The outstanding feature of much contemporary work here is that the information processing involved in mobile robotics—which is thought to contain important parallels to the neural processing of human perception, behavior, and cognition—relies on the environment as an indispensable tool in guiding the learning process. Robotics research, Clark wrote, "already demonstrates a variety of concrete ways in which perception and behavior productively interact via loops through action and the environment: loops that may now be considered as affording extra-neural opportunities for the minimization of prediction error."[395] In other words, the researchers who are interested in developing robots that are able to navigate their environment or perform particular tasks within that environment generally do not attempt to code an all-inclusive set of instructions. Instead, they provide programming that emphasizes heuristics that are rooted in robot-environment interactions. The robot's behavior evolves as it behaves in the environment, evaluates the results of that behavior in the context of the environmental inputs, and then behaves again. This dynamic loop between environment and behavior has been successful in creating robots that are able to learn and effectively complete numerous tasks.[396]

Another neuroscientist, Noë, suggested that the concept of an extended mind is, in fact, a logical result of neuroscientific methodology.[397] A fundamental unit of neuroscience is the neuron (though there are many types of neurons) and its function. However, quite some time ago, neuroscientists recognized that individual neurons acting alone will not provide explanations. Thus, neuroscientists study neurons as dynamic clusters that behave in particular ways over time. Given the expansion from studying single neurons to clusters, Noë wondered,

> But why stop there? It isn't as though brain function is transparent when we look to the dynamics of large-scale assemblies of cells. . . . Just as the fact that we cannot understand phenomena of consciousness in terms of the individual cell leads us to consider the causal powers of populations of cells, so the limits of what we can understand in terms of populations lead us to expand our conception and think of neural systems as elements of a larger system that includes the rest of the animal's body and also its situation in and interaction with the environment.[398]

Other neuroscientists have argued that neuroscientific research should abandon neuroessentialistic perspectives for reasons like those above. For instance, Dehaene described his neuroscientific training in the 1980s, in which consciousness—the "C word"—was not permitted during lab meetings and was incredibly rare in neuroscience publications.[399] He argued that it was widely believed that the concept of consciousness added nothing to scientific explanation and neuroscience would be better off abandoning it. However, Dehaene believed that many aspects of current and future neuroscience do not banish consciousness. New trends in neuroscience have incorporated a "key ingredient to the new science of consciousness: taking subjective reports seriously."[400] In fact, Dehaene argued that in the same way that behaviorism has been largely abandoned in favor of approaches that allow for the importance and explanatory power of consciousness, neuroscientific approaches to consciousness that have neglected subjectivity and self-reports may be neglected in the future.

Finally, some neuroscientists appear to agree with Graham's argument regarding the appropriate levels of explanation.[401] That is, some neuroscientists have argued that neuroscience has a prominent place in the investigation of psychology but that this place is within a particular domain. For instance, Carandini pointed out that a long-standing general rule in science is that scientists should operate at an appropriate level of description when using theories, forming hypotheses, and conducting experiments.[402] This means, for example, that when biologists think about, write about, and conduct experiments, they do not attempt to reduce their area of study to subatomic particles. In fact, they do not attempt to reduce their area of study to subatomic particles even if they agree that, in principle, biology can be reduced to chemistry and chemistry to physics. In other words:

> In physics . . . the equations for particle interactions become impossible to solve or even simulate once a system exceeds ten particles. So, to describe what a decent-sized piece of matter does, solid-state physicists developed remarkably successful theories operating at mesoscopic levels.[403]

Similarly, clinical psychologists have developed successful theories that operate at the psychological level, even if clinical psychologists agree that, in principle, psychology can be reduced to biology.

Clinical Considerations

The considerations discussed above are related to the negative consequences many authors have suggested essentialistic accounts of human experience and behavior may yield, whether that essentialism is described in chemical, biological, genetic, and/or neuronal terms. For example, Yanchar and Hill argued that an essentialistic approach to the mind "is problematic because it tends to predetermine what we take human nature to be without careful consideration of the consequences that this ontological commitment has for a variety of important issues" such as "intentionality, agency, morality, spirituality,

[and] the phenomenological essence of experience."[404] Dar-Nimrod and Heine argued that "essentialism may lead people to view outcomes as immutable and determined" when, in fact, this deterministic view is a drastic oversimplification.[405] Racine, Waldman, Rosenberg, and Illes worried that "neuro-realist and neuro-essentialist interpretations of neuroscience" have "far-reaching health and policy implications" such as "the credibility and availability of non-biological therapies."[406] Keyser and Nagel were concerned that "neurocentric accounts are likely to fuel 'naïve' notions of determinism that again might have detrimental psychological effects [by restricting] patients' perceived possibilities, like further forms of treatment beyond medication."[407] And Noë argued that it is "impossible to understand why people get depressed—or why this individual here and now is depressed—in neural terms alone" and attempting to do so ignores the importance of other factors.[408]

These concerns, though plausible, were not directly related to empirical investigations that substantiate them. However, a growing body of evidence strongly suggests that the concerns raised above are on target. Now, we will discuss this body of evidence, focusing on the studies that suggest that neuroessentialistic conceptions of depression have negative clinical effects.

Before turning to recent research on neuroessentialistic conceptions of depression, it is useful to note that there is substantial evidence that abstract ideas can affect beliefs, emotions, and behavior. For example, studies suggest that when individuals are exposed to information that supports or concludes that human beings do not have free will, those individuals are significantly more likely to behave aggressively,[409] cheat,[410] exhibit reduced self-control,[411] exhibit impaired cognitive ability to react to errors,[412] exhibit reduced processes related to agency,[413] and exhibit impaired intentional self-regulation.[414] In addition, they are more likely to hold racially prejudiced beliefs[415] and experience a reduction in the meaningfulness of life.[416] Considering the numerous studies demonstrating the negative effects of not believing in free will, Rigoni and Brass argued,

> Regardless of the philosophical question whether free will exists or not, it matters whether people believe in free will or not. Under this view, scientific positions that challenge the existence of free

will, such as neuroscientific reductionism, do not only have an important theoretical impact. They also have the potential to bring radical transformations of how laypersons consider themselves.[417]

If abstract concepts like free will can have impacts, neuroessentialistic conceptions of depression may do so as well, especially since one consequence of neuroessentialistic thinking is the belief that human beings do not possess free will.[418]

It is unlikely that free will or neuroessentialism are explicitly discussed in clinical settings. Nevertheless, neuroessentialistic conceptualizations of depression are deeply entrenched in thinking about mental health.[419] For example, the idea that depression is caused by a brain-based biological malfunction or pathology, usually described as a chemical imbalance, is present in the scientific literature,[420] public understanding,[421] information provided by mental health advocacy groups such as the National Alliance on Mental Illness,[422] and patients' conceptualization of their own depression.[423]

Could a neuroessentialistic conceptualization of depression have negative clinical consequences like the negative consequences of not believing in free will? Although this is a relatively new area of research, the evidence strongly suggests that it can. Below, the studies that examine the consequences of conceptualizing depression in a neuroessentialistic manner compared with a psychosocial manner are reviewed.

Deacon and Baird (2009)

Deacon and Baird recruited 90 college students and had them complete one of two possible questionnaires. The participants were randomly divided into two equal-sized groups, and each was given one of the questionnaires. Each questionnaire included three sections. In both questionnaires, the first section included demographic information and mental health history. The mental health history included questions aimed at determining whether the participant believed depression is primarily caused by biological or psychosocial factors. In both questionnaires, the second section asked the respondents to imagine that they felt depressed, sought professional help because of feeling depressed, and received a diagnosis of major depression.

Here the two questionnaires diverged. In the first version, a biological explanation was given before a biopsychosocial explanation. In the second version, this order was reversed. The biological explanation of depression contained information "adopted from the National Alliance on Mental Illness" website, which detailed the view that depression is caused by a chemical imbalance.[424] The biopsychosocial explanation of depression offered an alternative account of depression that emphasized that a wide variety of biological, psychological, and environmental influences were contributing causes of depression.

The third section of each questionnaire asked respondents questions about prognosis, stigma, and treatment. Questions in the prognosis portion included items such as, "To what extent would you feel able to effectively control the depression on your own?" and "To what extent would you expect your depression to be a chronic problem that persists for years?" Questions in the treatment portion included items such as, "How effective would you expect medication to be in treating your depression?" "How effective would you expect psychotherapy to be in treating your depression?" and "To what extent would you believe that making changes in your attitudes and lifestyle would improve your depression?"[425]

Deacon and Baird found statistically significant differences between the etiology of depression and stigma, prognosis, and treatment. Individuals who endorsed a biopsychosocial explanation of depression had a more positive prognosis and higher perceived efficacy of psychotherapy. Individuals who endorsed the biological explanation of depression had a more pessimistic prognosis and higher perceived efficacy of medication. The authors concluded that "compared to a biopsychosocial explanation, the chemical imbalance explanation . . . led to decreased personal and moral responsibility for depression, a worse expected prognosis, and the perception that psychosocial interventions are largely ineffective"[426]

Lebowitz, Ahn, and Nolen-Hoeksema (2013)

Lebowitz et al. conducted three studies. In the first two studies, participants ($N1$ = 108 and $N2$ = 40) were recruited online and then assessed for depression with a Beck Depression Inventory-II (BDI-II). Participants who obtained a score of at least 16 on the BDI-II rated their level of agreement with 10 causes of their depressive symptoms, including biochemical and genetic explanations of their symptoms (7-point Likert-type scale from *very unlikely* to *very likely*). These participants were then instructed to answer questions about their expected duration of symptoms. The authors conducted a linear regression and found that "the more people with depressive symptoms attribute those symptoms to genetic and biochemical causes, the longer they tend to expect their symptoms to last."[427]

The third study was the same as the first two but included participants who did not obtain a score of 16 or above on the BDI-II and the inclusion of an additional portion. In this added portion, the participants were randomly assigned to one of three conditions: malleable, biological-illness, and control. In the malleable condition, participants watched a six-minute video that "provided a basic primer on epigenetics," which emphasized that environmental factors can modify the biology of mood.[428] For example, the video detailed that exercise and sunlight alter brain chemistry in a way that alleviates the symptoms of depression. In the biological-illness condition, participants watched a different six-minute video that provided information about depression that was like accounts portrayed in scientific and popular literature. This information highlighted that depression often runs in families and that research has shown that there are differences between the brains of depressed and nondepressed individuals. The control condition participants did not view a video. Then, the participants were asked to rate their expectations of prognosis, personal agency in relationship to mood, and outlook for the future.

Regression analyses found that "biochemical/genetic attribution scores were a significant predictor of longer expected symptoms duration and lower perceived odds of recovery."[429] Importantly, Lebowitz et al. also found that the malleability condition was effective in reducing prognostic pessimism as well as in increasing optimistic thinking and personal agency in relationship to mood. The authors concluded that "given the increasing prevalence of biomedical conceptualizations of depression, the notion that depressed individuals who hold such beliefs might be more vulnerable to pessimism about the course of their disorder is alarming."[430]

Read, Cartwright, Gibson, Sheils, and Haslam (2014)

Read et al. conducted a study in which 1,829 individuals, who had all been prescribed antidepressants in the past five years and were at least 18 years old, answered an online questionnaire. The questionnaire had 47 items and included yes-no, Likert-type scale, and open-ended formats. The questionnaire inquired into several different areas associated with antidepressants, prescriptions, pharmaceutical companies, and beliefs about the causes of depression. The authors stated that the key question of their study was, "There are many theories, and lots of debate, about what causes problems like depression. Please indicate the extent to which you think the following factors are causes of depression in general."[431] This question was followed by 17 items, gathered from scientific literature, which listed biological, psychological, and social causes. Participants were instructed to answer each of these items on a five-point, Likert-type scale from strongly disagree to strongly agree.

Several different relationships were identified between causal beliefs about depression and use of antidepressants, interaction with the prescriber, perceived efficacy of antidepressants, and other factors. Importantly, Read et al. "replicated the many previous findings" that "bio-genetic beliefs" about depression were associated with greater prognostic pessimism.[432] This finding was based on a regression analysis of causal beliefs, and the item from the questionnaire read, "People cannot get better by themselves even if they try."[433] The authors concluded that their study "replicated the many previous findings that bio-genetic beliefs are associated with prognostic pessimism."[434]

Kemp, Lickel, and Deacon (2014)

Kemp et al. conducted a study of 73 participants who reported presently or previously experiencing a depressive episode assessed via an online screening item. Participants were randomized into two groups: the chemical imbalance condition ($N = 37$) and the control condition ($N = 36$).

The participants in both conditions were individually administered the credible but fake "Rapid Depression Test" (RDT), which was described to the participants as a test that "would allow participants to determine whether or not their depressive episode(s) were caused by a chemical imbalance in the brain."[435] This test included an "experimenter" (an undergraduate research assistant) wearing a lab coat swabbing the inside of each participant's cheek and then placing the swab in a container. The experimenter then explained to each participant that he was leaving the room to conduct the lab analysis on the swab. After 10 minutes, the experimenter returned with the results of the RDT and explained them to the participant.

In the chemical imbalance condition, the experimenter explained to the participant that the RDT indicated that his or her depressive episode was "caused by an imbalance in the neurotransmitter serotonin."[436] Each participant was then shown a bar graph illustrating normal levels of neurotransmitters with the exception of serotonin, which was far below the indicated normative range. In the control condition, the procedure was identical except that the experimenter explained that the test results indicated that all of each person's neurotransmitter levels were within the normative range.

After being presented with the results, each participant completed four assessments: Causal Attributions for Depression Scale, Perceptions of Depression Scale, Negative Mood Regulation Scale, and the Credibility and Expectancy Questionnaire. These scales were meant to collectively measure themes such as the participant's understanding of the causes of their depression, perception of stigma, prognostic pessimism, and expected mood regulation.

After the experiment was conducted, the participants were debriefed. The debriefing included an explanation that the RDT is not a valid test and the administration of a fifth assessment, the Deception Credibility Questionnaire. The Deception Credibility Questionnaire is designed to measure "the credibility of the manipulation."[437]

Between-group comparisons found that there was a significant difference in prognostic pessimism and mood regulation expectancies with the chemical imbalance condition having greater prognostic pessimism and lower mood regulation expectancies. A repeated-measures analysis of variance (ANOVA) found that "participants in the chemical imbalance condition rated pharmacotherapy as more credible than psychotherapy."[438] Those in the chemical imbalance condition also believed that pharmacotherapy would be more effective than psychotherapy. Kemp et al. concluded:

> Chemical imbalance test feedback increased prognostic pessimism, lowered negative mood regulation expectancies, and led participants to view pharmacotherapy as more credible and effective than psychotherapy. . . . The present findings suggest that providing individuals with a chemical imbalance causal explanation for their depressive symptoms . . . activates a host of negative beliefs with the potential to worsen the course of depression and attenuate response to treatment, particularly psychotherapy.[439]

Schroder, Dawood, Yalch, Donnellan, and Moser (2014)

Schroder et al. conducted two studies that were designed to measure the relationship between participants' implicit theories of emotions, such as anxiety and depression, and three domains: psychological symptoms, emotion regulation, and treatment choice.

Following previous research, Schroder et al. described two types of implicit theories: entity theory and incremental theory. Entity theory holds that "abilities and traits" are "relatively set-in-stone and unable to change," and those that hold entity theory "typically attribute their capacities to genetic and biological causes."[440] On the other hand, incremental theory holds that "self-attributes are responsive to improvement and growth with learning and effort" and that these attributes can be modified by "motivation and effort."[441]

In the first study, Schroder et al. attempted to measure "how implicit theories" of anxiety, intelligence, and emotion related to a number of different outcome measures, including depression, emotion regulation, and "hypothetical treatment preferences."[442] Participants ($N = 388$) were assessed with three implicit theory measures: the implicit theories of intelligence, the implicit theories of emotion, and the implicit theories of anxiety. These protocols are designed to measure a participant's views on the ability to control and change intelligence and emotion. Participants were also assessed with several other instruments such as the Penn State Worry Questionnaire, the Mood and Anxiety Symptom Questionnaire, the BDI-II, the Emotion

Regulation Questionnaire, and an item measuring hypothetical treatment choice.

Schroder et al. found that the implicit theory of emotion scale "significantly predicted many of the" mental health symptoms assessed, such as depression.[443] Furthermore, the incremental theory of emotion scale was "uniquely associated with more cognitive reappraisal" suggesting that individuals who endorse incremental theory more than entity theory are more likely to participate in attempts to reframe their emotional experience. This is important because reframing emotional experience is often an effective strategy for reducing negative psychological symptoms. Finally, the authors found that participants whose implicit theories of emotions were "indicative of more of an entity theory" were significantly more likely to choose medication instead of psychotherapy as a hypothetical treatment choice, which suggests that these participants expect medication to be more beneficial.[444]

Like the first study, the second study ($N = 298$) found that incremental theories of emotion were "negatively related to symptoms of anxiety [and] depression . . . and positively related to cognitive reappraisal."[445]

Schroder et al. concluded that "cultivation of incremental theories of . . . emotion may be most beneficial in terms of mental health and functioning"[446] and that "changing implicit theories more toward incremental beliefs may lead to reductions in symptoms."[447] In other words, believing that one's emotional state is fixed via genetic or biological causes is related to less cognitive reappraisal and worse mental health symptoms.

Lebowitz and Ahn (2014)

Lebowitz and Ahn conducted three studies that focused on clinicians instead of patients. In the first two studies ($N1 = 132$ and $N2 = 105$), mental health clinicians were given vignettes that described patients with mental disorders. The first study described patients with schizophrenia and social phobia. The second study described patients with major depression and obsessive-compulsive disorder. Each disorder was described in two separate passages. One passage described the disorder from a genetic and neurobiological perspective.

The other passage described the disorder from a psychosocial perspective. Each mental health clinician was given a total of four vignettes in which both disorders were described from both perspectives mentioned above. After reading each of the vignettes, how the clinicians "felt about the fictitious patients" was measured by having them view 18 adjectives and then rate "how much each one described their feelings toward the patient described."[448] This method is "well-validated" and "extensively used in empathy research."[449]

In addition to measuring empathy, the clinicians also rated how much improvement they expected each of the patients to make via medication or psychotherapy as well as the "clinical utility" of each descriptive passage. The data indicated that biological explanations resulted in significantly less clinician empathy than the psychosocial explanation in both studies. Furthermore, in both studies, biological explanations were evaluated as less clinically useful for each disorder except schizophrenia, and, also in both studies, clinicians rated psychotherapy as significantly less effective than medication when a biological explanation was given versus when a psychosocial explanation was given.

In the third study ($N = 106$), participants were given both biological and psychosocial explanations of psychological disorders, but one form of explanation was dominant. They believed this would "more closely mirror the real world, in which biological conceptualizations of psychopathology may gradually come to predominate psychosocial explanations without totally eliminating them."[450] Similar to the first two studies, descriptive passages in which biological explanations dominated resulted in significantly less clinician empathy than passages in which psychosocial explanations and biologically dominant explanations led to "significantly higher ratings of medication effectiveness and significantly lower ratings of psychotherapy effectiveness."[451] The study by Lebowitz and Ahn concluded by stating that the data suggest that "biological explanations of mental illness can have clinically relevant negative consequences among mental health clinicians," especially decreasing clinician empathy and increasing clinician expectancy that patients could benefit from psychotherapy.[452]

Concluding Thoughts and Discussion

The studies examined suggest that beliefs about the etiology of depression have tangible clinical effects. Perhaps most importantly, the more an individual believes that depression is caused by biological factors, the greater his or her prognostic pessimism. Conceptualization of depression is also related to treatment preferences and mood regulation. These findings are congruent with other studies that have explored the effect of biogenetic explanations of other psychological disorders.[453]

A large body of research has shown that an individual's expectancies about treatment outcomes have a significant effect on his or her actual treatment outcome. In addition to client expectancies, clinician expectancies for client improvement also have a significant impact on treatment outcomes, and thus conceptualizations of depression that decrease clinician expectancies will likely worsen treatment outcomes.[454]

Nevertheless, this research does not provide evidence of the effect size that biogenetic etiologies of depression have on client treatment outcomes. Thus, although there will almost certainly be some negative effects of biogenetic etiologies, how large those effects are remains to be identified.

Despite these limitations, a plausible recommendation for clinicians is to be *aware* of these theoretical and clinical concerns and be ready to share that information with their clients so that clients can make an informed decision about their treatment. Blease[455] argued that this entails clinicians informing clients that the evidence suggests that depression is a complicated phenomenon that is not entirely understood by either scientists or mental health professionals, that there is evidence to think that depression may not be explained by neuroessentialistic etiologies such as the chemical imbalance hypothesis, and that neuroessentialistic etiologies may hinder treatment outcomes.[456]

Conclusion
Courage Over Chemistry

In the preceding chapters, I detailed philosophical, scientific, and clinical arguments that challenged common biogenetic etiologies of mental disorders.

Here at the end, after reading over these essays as a set, a new idea has emerged.

Although my opinion on the arguments given previously has not substantially changed since I wrote them, the more I reflect on my concerns, the more I've become convinced that my primary objection to biogenetic etiologies is not necessarily an objection rooted in science or in philosophy.

Rather, my objection is rooted in *ethics*.

Let me illustrate this with a short story.

In 2007, I began experiencing symptoms of obsessive-compulsive disorder (OCD). OCD is a severe mental disorder, characterized by intrusive, obsessive thoughts which cause extreme anxiety. This anxiety motivates compulsive behavior. For instance, an obsessive thought, such as: "What if I left the stove on?"—is followed by the compulsion to check that the stove is on, or off. However, the compulsive behaviors usually only reduce anxiety for a short time. The obsessive thought returns, followed by the anxiety, followed by the compulsive behavior. "Did I really shut the stove off? I better check again." You check again. "Am I *absolutely* sure the stove is off?" You check again. This pattern often escalates, taking up more and more of each day, often many hours. In severe cases, the obsessive-compulsive cycle can take up most of the day.

As is common for those suffering from OCD, I didn't understand what I was experiencing.

I felt afraid and ashamed.

I didn't seek help for years. And when I did, I wasn't convinced by the treatment advice I was given.

This experience motivated me to begin studying clinical psychology, eventually beginning a doctoral program. During this time, I realized I was suffering from OCD and I thoroughly researched the best available treatment options. Despite what I'd been repeatedly told—that I had a chemical imbalance in my brain and that I'd likely need medication for the rest of my life—the clinical literature identified a form of psychotherapy called "exposure and response prevention" (ERP) that looked like it would provide me the best chance to feel better.

And I wanted to feel better.

ERP entailed exposing myself to anxiety-producing situations, then resisting the urge to reduce my anxiety via compulsive behaviors. So, for instance, ERP could include my *deliberately* standing next to my stove before leaving my house, and *deliberately* abstaining from checking the stove before leaving, and then *deliberately* not going back to check after I'd left.

ERP is straightforward and easy to understand. But "conceptual understanding" is not the same as "real world application." Due to the nature of my obsessive thoughts and their attending anxiety, refraining from my compulsive behaviors, as ERP recommended, felt like walking into the mouth of death.

It was during these moments that *courage* became central to my life.

Over and beyond the conditioning and reinforcement processes involved, at a foundational level, ERP is about *the willingness to risk*. Taking risks is hard. It's always possible, even if only logically conceivable, that my intrusive thoughts might be right. In other words, I may indeed have left the stove on. At the same time, with ERP I began to realize that I could begin to trust myself. I began to believe that I could trust myself. More specifically, I began to believe that if I didn't begin trusting myself sometime, then my whole life would be pulled into a never-ending whirlpool of obsessions and compulsions. But I had to take the risk. I had to be courageous.

Finding courage offered me an alternative path. It allowed me to reply to my intrusive thoughts: "You might be right. I can't know for sure. But if I don't begin trusting myself, how will I ever move beyond my current struggles? I trust myself."

And what's more, courage allowed me to see that my worst fear wasn't my house burning down because I'd left the stove on, or any of the other nightmares intruding upon my mind.

My worst fear was that I'd live my whole life *governed* by these fears.

My worst fear was that I'd miss my chance to be brave.

So I took my chance. I took the risk.

And—surprisingly, quickly—my life changed for the better.

From the point of view of ethics, biogenetic etiologies diminish or remove the motivation to develop courage. It's not courageous to "think positive and walk-it-out" when you have a broken leg. That makes little sense—because walking around on a broken leg, thinking happy thoughts will make my leg worse. Psychotherapy won't heal my bones. Likewise, if my anxiety is the result of my "broken brain," then what biogenetic etiologists tell me is that I need a "cast" (e.g., psychiatric medication).

But there's no evidence my anxiety was caused by a broken brain and there's plenty of evidence that I had the power to understand my situation, to make decisions, and to change.

This is why it's so important for me to share this truth: The evidence supporting biogenetic etiologies is dangerous. Alternatively, the evidence that individuals can powerfully alter their internal experiences via courageous use of cognitive-behavioral therapy—and other similar techniques, like ERP—is strong. But it takes courage to accept this reality and take a risk for yourself and the people you love.

This way of looking at my experiences opens many questions: What is courage? What does its application entail? For the sake of what—or whom—is courage practiced? What dangers are associated with it and what can get in its way? I don't have answers to these questions. But even without them, I've seen the power of asking and I'll continue to do so—as long as I'm willing to take the risk.

Endnotes

Chapter 1. Child-Centered Play Therapy

1   Frankl V., *Man's Search for Meaning*. Beacon Press, Boston, MA, 2014 p. 118.
2   This is a fictional case study based upon elements commonly found in my clinical work.
3   Friedberg & McClure, 2015
4   Stagnitti, 2004; Fagen, 1981
5   Lillard, 2015
6   Smith, 1997
7   Pelligrini & Smith, 1998
8   Pellegrini & Smith, 1998
9   Huizinga, 1950
10   Nicolopoulou, 2010
11   Whitebread, Coltman, Jameson, & Lander, 2009
12   Nicolopoulou, 2010, p. 2
13   Sarama & Clements, 2009
14   Fisher, Hirsh-Pasek, Newcombe, & Glinka, 2013
15   Blanco, Ray, & Holliman, 2012
16   Linsey & Colwell, 2003
17   Newton & Jenvey, 2011
18   O'Connor, 2000
19   Crenshaw & Kenney-Noziska, 2014
20   Axline, 1969, p. 16
21   Gil, 1991
22   Gaskill & Perry, 2014
23   Turns & Kimmes, 2014
24   Axline, 1969, p. 15
25   Axline, 1969, p. 15
26   Ethical guidelines and state laws prohibit the "unconditional acceptance" of behavior that poses significant risk of injury to self or others.
27   O'Connor, 2000
28   O'Connor, 2000
29   Bratton, Rhine & Jones, 2005
30   Ryan & Edge, 2012
31   Schaefer & Drewes, 2013
32   Wampold & Imel, 2015
33   Drewes & Schaefer, 2013b
34   Welzel & Inglehart, 2010
35   Deci & Ryan, 2000
36   Wampold & Imel, 2015
37   Bennett & Eberts, 2013, p. 34

38   Bennett & Eberts, 2013, p. 23

39   Korpela, Kyttä, & Hartig, 2002

40   Bandura, 1991; Wrosch et al., 2003

41   Yeager & Yeager, 2013

42   Berk, Mann & Ogan, 2006; Elias & Berk, 2002

43   Drewes & Schaefer, 2013a

44   Ogawa, 2004

45   Drewes & Schaefer, 2013a

46   Leblanc & Ritchie, 2001

47   Wampold & Imel, 2015

48   Bratton, Ray, Rhine & Jones, 2005

49   Cohen, 1988

50   Ray, Armstrong, Balkin & Jayne, 2015

51   Lin & Bratton, 2015

52   Bratton, 2016

53   Casey et al., 2013

54   Ross, 2013

55   Insel, 2015

56   Insel et al., 2010

57   For instance, it is hoped that the RDoC can solve an important
        problem with the *DSM-5*. Many *DSM-5* diagnostic categories have
        difficulty obtaining consistent diagnoses from multiple clinicians.
        That is, different clinicians frequently diagnose the same client
        with a different *DSM-5* diagnosis. Another motivation is related to
        the emphasis on precision medicine in medical fields.

58   Deacon, 2013; Kendler, 2005; Walter, 2013

59   Noordermeer, Luman, & Oosterlaan, 2016

60   Abramovitch & Schweiger, 2015; Lilienfeld, 2014; Lilienfeld &
        Treadway, 2016; Paris & Kirmayer, 2016

61   Lilienfield, 2014, p. 132

62   Fuchs, 2011

63   Whooley, 2014

64   Lebowitz, 2014; Read, Cartwright, Gibson, Shiels, & Haslam, 2014;
        It is almost certainly true that other principal factors influence the
        emphasis on medication over psychosocial interventions, such
        as the power and influence of pharmaceutical companies and
        the relative lesser emphasis placed on psychosocial intervention
        research for psychiatric disorders. Nevertheless, the reliance on
        medication is pervasive and importantly linked to biological
        etiologies.

65   Fulton et al., 2009

66   Visser et al., 2016

67   Sohn, Moga, Blumenschein, & Talbert, 2016

68   Coleman, Walker, Lee, Friesen, & Squire, 2009

69   Johnston, Seipp, Hommersen, Hoza, & Fine, 2005

70   Wedge, 2016

71   Note that the rate of diagnosis appears similar in both countries; it is the prevalence of various treatments that is different.

72   I limit my discussion here to ADHD medication. It should be noted, though, that antidepressant and antipsychotic medication also commonly have significant negative side effects, sometimes terribly severe ones.

73   Shin, Roughead, Park, & Pratt, 2016

74   Cortese et al., 2013; Konofal, Lecendreaux, & Cortese, 2010; MacKenzie et al., 2016; Schwartz et al., 2014

75   Bourgeois, Kim, & Mandl, 2014

76   Baggerly, Ray, & Bratton, 2010; Fedewa et al., 2016; Pelham, Jr. et al., 2000; Pelham, Jr. & Fabiano, 2008; Ray, Bratton, Rhine, & Jones, 2001; Weisz, McCarty, & Valeri, 2006

77   Crystal et al., 2016

Chapter 2. Mental Disorders and Genetics

78   Beck & Dozois, 2011

79   Beck, 1963; Ellis, 1962

80   Lebowitz, 2014

81   Racine et al., 2013

82   Deacon, 2013, p. 784.

83   Gratten, Wray, Keller, & Visscher, 2014

84   Ripke et al., 2013, p. 497

85   Racine et al., 2013

86   Racine et al., 2013

87   Joseph, 2014

88   Jackson, 1960

89   Jackson, 1960

90   Joseph, 2001

91   Joseph, 2014; For those interested, Joseph discussed psychiatric research and twin studies in exhaustive detail.

92   Panofsky, 2014

93   Panofsky, 2014, loc. 2839

94   Panofsky, 2014, loc. 2839

95   Ferdman, 2015

Chapter 3. Mental Disorders and Brain Scan Research

96   British Psychological Society, 2013

97   International Society for Ethical Psychology and Psychiatry, 2013

98   American Psychiatric Association, 2013

99   Insel, 2013

100   Kupfer, 2013

101   Whitaker & Cosgrove, 2015

102   Insel, 2013

103   e.g., Douaud et al., 2007

104   Howell et al., 2013

105   Eluvathingal et al., 2006

106   Akdeniz et al., 2014

107   Andreasen, Liu, Ziebell, Vora, & Ho, 2013; Szeszko et al., 2014

108   e.g., Gogtay, 2008; Gogtay & Rapoport, 2008

109   e.g., Khandaker et al., 2015; Papakostas et al., 2013; Raison & Miller, 2011

110   Read, Fosse, Moskowitz, & Perry, 2014; Read, Perry, Moskowitz, & Connolly, 2001; van der Kolk, 2003

111   Epel et al., 2004; Labonté et al., 2012

112   e.g., van der Kolk, 2003

113   Brown et al., 2014; Dorrington et al., 2014; Janssen et al., 2004

114   Neville et al., 2013

115   Abbass, Nowoweiski, Bernier, Tarzwell, & Beutel, 2014; Roffman, Gerber, & Click, 2012

116   Hölzel et al., 2010

117   ten Brinke et al., 2015

118   Deckersbach et al., 2014

119   e.g., Deacon, 2013; Whitaker, 2010

120   Frances, 2014, p. 47

121   Frances, 2014, p. 48

122   Phillips, 2014, p. 40

123   Lebowitz & Ahn, 2014

124   Andrews, Thomson, Amstadter, & Neale, 2012

125   Moncrieff, 2013a

126   Fava, Getty, Belaise, Guidi, & Offidani, 2015; Nielsen, Hansen, & Gøtzsche, 2012

127   Hyman & Nestler, 1996

128   Whitaker, 2010

129   Khan, Faucett, Lichtenberg, Kirsch, & Brown, 2012

130   Harrow, Jobe, & Faull, 2012; Wunderink, Nieboer, Wiersma, Sytema, & Nienhuis, 2013

Chapter 4. Depression and the Chemical Imbalance Hypothesis

131   Lebowitz, Ahn, & Nolen-Hoeksema, 2013

132   Park & Ahn, 2013

133   Herculano-Houzel, 2009

134   Baumeister, Hawkins, & Uzelac, 2003; Leo & Lacasse, 2008; Kirsch, 2014a

135   Mulinari, 2012

136   Goldberg, Bell, & Pollard, 2014

137   Healy, 1997

138   Crane, 1956

139   Loomer et al., 1957

140 Loomer et al., 1957, p. 130

141 Loomer et al., 1957

142 Cole et al., 1959; Robie, 1958

143 Kirsch, 2010, p. 84

144 Kuhn, 1958

145 Kuhn, 1958, p. 459

146 Valenstein, 1998

147 Ball & Kiloh, 1959

148 Moncrieff, 2008

149 Kirsch, 2010

150 Moncrieff, 2008

151 Schildkraut, 1965

152 Coppen, 1967

153 Platt & Sears, 1956; Winsor, 1954

154 Freis, 1954; Kass & Brown, 1955; Lemieux, Davignon, & Genest, 1956

155 Baumeister et al., 2003

156 Kirsch, 2010, p. 87

157 Schildkraut, 1965, p. 519

158 Kirsch, 2010; Moncrief, 2008; Valenstein, 1988

159 Almasi, Stafford, Kravitz, & Mansfield, 2006; Huxley, 1932

160 Kirsch, 2010, p. 90

161 Niehoff, Palacios, & Kuhar, 1979

162 Mendels & Frazer, 1974

163 Mendels & Frazer, 1974; Kirsch, 2010

164 Ruhé, Mason, & Schene, 2007, p. 354

165 Rogers & Pies, 2008, p. 32

166 Breedlove, Rosenzweig, & Watson, 2007

167 Healy & Savage, 1998; Baumeister et al., 2003

168 Healy & Savage, 1998, p. 337

169 Healy & Savage, 1998, p. 377

170 Baumeister et al., 2003

171 Baumeister et al., 2003, p. 207

172 Healy, 1997; Valenstein, 1998

173 Baumeister et al., 2003, p. 207

174 Baumeister et al., 2003, p. 216

175 Baumeister et al., 2003

176 Nabeshima & Kim, 2013

177 Healy & Savage, 1998

178 Baumeister et al., 2003

179 Coplan, Gopinath, Abdallah, & Berry, 2014; Kirsch, 2010

180 Coplan et al., 2014, p. 7

181 Kirsch, 2010, p. 97

182 Kirsch, 2008, 2010, 2014; Kirsch, Moore, Scoboria, & Nicholls, 2002; Kirsch & Sapirstein, 1998

183 Kirsch, 2010

184	Scott, 2012
185	Kirsch, 1985, 1999
186	Kirsch, 1997b, 2010
187	Kirsch, 2010, p. 2
188	Kirsch & Sapirstein, 1998
189	Kirsch, 2010, p. 11
190	Kirsch, 2010, p. 11
191	Kirsch, 2010, p. 12
192	Kirsch, 2010, p. 12
193	Kirsch, 2010, p. 13
194	Kirsch, 2010, p. 15
195	Kirsch, 2010, p. 19
196	Kirsch, 2010, p. 20
197	Kirsch, 2010, p. 20
198	Kirsch, 2010, p. 20
199	Kirsch, 2010, p. 18
200	Kirsch, 2010
201	Klein, 1998
202	Kirsch, 2010, p. 24
203	Kirsch, 2010
204	Kirsch, 2010
205	Melander, Ahlqvist-Rastad, Meijer, & Beermann, 2003, p. 1173
206	Kirsch, 2010, p. 24
207	Kirsch, 2010
208	Kirsch, 2010, p. 26
209	Kirsch et al., 2002, p. 7
210	Johnson & Kirsch, 2008; Leucht et al., 2013; Moncrieff, 2013b; Moncrieff & Kirsch, 2005
211	Kirsch, 2010, p. 37
212	Barbui, Furukawa, & Cipriani, 2008; Fountoulakis & Möller, 2011; Fournier et al., 2010; Huedo-Medina, Johnson, & Kirsch, 2012; Ioannidis, 2008; Khan, Faucett, Lichtenberg, Kirsch, & Brown, 2012; Khan, Leventhal, Khan, & Brown, 2002; Kirsch et al., 2008; Turner, Matthews, Linardatos, Tell, & Rosenthal, 2008
213	Khin et al., 2011
214	Kirsch, 2014a, p. 129
215	Kirsch, 2010, p. 81
216	Mulinari, 2012; Whitaker, 2011
217	Leo & Lacasse, 2008
218	Leo & Lacasse, 2008
219	Kirsch, 2010, p. 50
220	Kirsch, 2010
221	Kirsch, 2010
222	Szasz, 1974

223   Andrews, Thomson, Amstadter, & Neale, 2012; Breggin, 2001; Spielmans & Kirsch, 2014a

Chapter 5. Depression and Feminism

224   Hyman, 2010.
225   Hurst & Genest, 1995; Weissman, Bland, & Canino, 1996.
226   Shanmugasegaram, Russell, Kovacs, Stewart, & Grace, 2012.
227   Currie, 2005; Pratt, Brody, & Gu, 2011.
228   Henningsen, 2015.
229   Monroe & Anderson, 2015.
230   Durisko, Mulsant, & Andrews, 2015.
231   Kessler & Bromet, 2013.
232   Schwartz & Petersen, 2016.
233   Cabaniss, Moga, & Oquendo, 2015.
234   Lilienfeld & Treadway, 2016.
235   Lacasse & Leo, 2015.
236   Schultz, 2015a.
237   Steen, 1991
238   e.g., Horney, 1967/1993.
239   Henwood & Pidgeon, 1995.
240   Hurst & Genest, 1995.
241   Stoppard, 1999; Ussher, 2010.
242   Lafrance, 2009.
243   Hankin & Abramson, 2001, p. 785.
244   Stark & Flitcraft, 1988.
245   Bondi & Burman, 2001; Chantler, 2005; Cole, 2009; Penfold & Walker, 1984.
246   Stark & Flitcraft, 1988.
247   Mowbray, Herman, & Hazel, 1992; Steen, 1991.
248   e.g., Sands, 1996.
249   Kichuk, Lebowitz, & Adams, 2015; Lebowitz, 2014; Schultz, 2015b.
250   Kemp, Lickel, & Deacon, 2014; Schultz, 2015b.
251   Alladin, 2013; Constantino, 2012; Constantino, Ametrano, & Greenberg, 2012; Tambling, 2012.
252   Mowbray et al., 1992; Steen, 1991.
253   Gammell & Stoppard, 1999.
254   Gammell & Stoppard, 1999.

Chapter 6. Explaining Depression in Clinical Settings

255   Pies, 2014
256   Davies, 2010, para. 52
257   Lebowitz, Ahn, & Nolen-Hoeksema, 2013
258   Read, Cartwright, Gibson, Shiels, and Magliano, 2015

259   Cohen & Hughes, 2011; Fosgerau & Davidsen, 2014; Fullagar & O'Brien, 2014; Gibson, Cartwright, & Read, 2016; MacKay & Rutherford, 2012; O'Brien, 2012

260   Buchman, Borgelt, Whiteley, & Illes, 2013, p. 71

261   Pies, 2011, p. 1

262   Lacasse &Leo, 2015

263   Lacasse &Leo, 2015

264   Deacon & Baird, 2009; see also, Lacasse & Leo, 2005

265   Arpaly, 2005; McMullen & Sigurdson, 2014

266   American Diabetes Association, 2014

267   Insel, 2015, p. 5; see also Deacon, 2013

268   Ross, 2013

269   Venkatasubramanian & Keshavan, 2016

270   Fried, 2015

271   ADA, 2014

272   BDI; Beck, Steer, & Carbin, 1988

273   HRSD; Hamilton, 1960

274   APA, 2013

275   Zimmerman, Ellison, Young, Chelminski, & Dalrymple, 2014

276   Zimmerman et al., 2014

277   APA

278   Fried et al., 2016

279   Fried et al., 2016

280   DAFNE Study Group, 2002; Ehrmann, Bergis-Jurgan, Haak, Kulzer, & Hermanns, 2016

281   Beck & Alford, 2009; Ellis, 1987; Teasdale, Segal, & Williams, 1995; Young, Klosko, & Weishaar, 2003

282   Cuijpers, Berking, Andersson, Quigley, Kleiboer, & Dobson, 2013; Wampold & Imel, 2015

283   Kirsch, 2010

284   Moncrieff, Wessely, & Hardy, 2004; Rutherford et al., 2016

285   Moncrieff & Kirsch, 2015

286   Fullagar, 2009; LaFrance, 2007; Lafrance & McKenzie-Mohr, 2013

287   Fullagar, 2009, p. 395

288   Gibson, Cartwright, & Read, 2016

289   Gibson, Cartwright, & Read, p.3

290   Angermeyer, Holzinger, Carta, & Schomerus, 2011, p. 367

291   Hansell et al., 2011

292   See also: Harris, 2009; Rose, 2013

293   Insel, 2015

294   APA, 2013; Ross, 2013

295   AMA, 2016; Blease, 2014

296   Buchman et al., 2013; Cohen & Hughes, 2011; Deacon & Baird, 2009; Iselin & Addis, 2003; Kemp, Lickel, & Deacon, 2014; Khalsa, McCarthy, Sharpless, Barrett, & Barber, 2011; Kuppin & Carpiano, 2008; Lebowitz, Rosenthal, & Ahn, 2012; Marsh & Romano, 2016

297   Andrews, Thomson, Amstadter, & Neale, 2012
298   Andrews et al.; Carvalho, Sharma, Brunoni, Vieta, & Fava, 2016
299   Carvalho et al., 2016
300   Moncrieff, 2016
301   Andrews et al., 2012, p. 13
302   Carvalho et al., 2016, p. 281
303   Cuijpers et al., 2013; De Maat, Dekker, Schoevers, & De Jonghe, 2006; Gartlehner et al., 2015; Khan, Faucett, Lichtenberg, Kirsch & Brown, 2012; Margraf & Schneider, 2016
304   Garlehner et al., 2015, p. 81
305   De Matt et al., 2006
306   Khan et al., 2012
307   Lebowitz & Ahn, 2015
308   Farrell, Lee, & Deacon, 2015
309   Schmidt, Brown, McClelland, Glennon, & Mountford, 2016

Chapter 7. Mental Disorders and Stigma

310   Holmes, 2016
311   Corrigan, Druss, & Perlick, 2014
312   Bring Change 2 Mind, 2016
313   Corrigan et al., 2000, p. 53
314   Bring Change 2 Mind, 2016
315   Insel, 2015, p. 5
316   Deacon, 2013; Fuchs, 2012; Graham, 2013; Miller, 2010
317   Fuchs, 2011
318   Hunter & Schultz, 2016
319   Månsson et al., 2016
320   Kendler, 2005, p. 435
321   Kendler, 2005, p. 434
322   Kendler, 2005, p. 434
323   Angermeyer et al., 2014, p. 702
324   Kvaale, Gottdiener, & Haslam, 2013; Schomerus, Matschinger, & Angermeyer, 2014; Speerforck, Schomerus, Pruess, & Angermeyer, 2014
325   Wiesjahn, Jung, Kremser, Rief, & Lincoln, 2016
326   Schomerus et al., 2014, p. 311
327   Corrigan et al., 2014.

Chapter 8. Neuroessentialism

328   Ghaemi, 2010, p. ix; see also Borrell-Carrió, Suchman, & Epstein, 2004; Cabaniss, Moga, & Oquendo, 2015; Hatala, 2012; McLaren, 1998; Van Oudenhove & Cuypers, 2014
329   Reiner, 2011, p. 161
330   Rowlands, 2010, p. 2

331	Satel & Lilienfeld, 2013, p. ix
332	Satel & Lilienfeld, 2013, p. ix
333	Frazzetto & Anker, 2009, p. 815
334	Bentall, 2006
335	Bentall, 2006, p. 222
336	Zachar, 2000, p. 33
337	Müller, Fletcher, & Steinberg, 2006
338	Ghaemi, 2013
339	Gruen, 1998, p. 85
340	Gold & Stoljar, 1999, p. 810
341	Choudhury & Slaby, 2011
342	Racine, 2015
343	Ross, 2013, p. 195
344	Insel, 2013, para. 2
345	Insel, 2014, p. 397
346	Walter, 2013, p. 4
347	Insel, 2013, para. 7
348	Wakefield, 2014, p. 39
349	Whitaker, 2011
350	Pincus et al., 1998, p. 528
351	Olfson & Marcus, 2009, p. 850
352	Kirsch, 2010; Pratt, Brody, & Gu, 2011
353	Pratt et al., 2011
354	Park & Grow, 2008
355	Lacasse & Leo, 2005; Leo & Lacasse, 2008
356	Park & Grow, 2008
357	Deacon, 2013
358	Hyman, 2012
359	Fuchs, 2011; Horst, 2012; Vintiadis, 2014
360	Gold & Stoljar, 1999
361	Graham, 2013, p. 87
362	Graham, 2013
363	Graham, 2013
364	McInerney, Mellor, & Nicholas, 2013
365	McInerney et al., 2013
366	Graham, 2013
367	Noë, 2009
368	Dretske, 2004
369	Moore & Fresco, 2012; Sloman, Price, Gilbert, & Gardner, 2004; Watkins & Teasdale, 2004; Wolpert, 2008
370	Bennett, Dennett, Hacker, & Searle, 2009
371	Bennett et al., 2009
372	Bennett et al., 2009, p. 136
373	Rogers, 1967, p. 45
374	Rogers, 1967, p. 45
375	Frankl, 1978, 1980; Längle & Sykes, 2006

376	Frankl, 1980, p. 15
377	Frankl, 1980, p. 16
378	Cabaniss et al., 2015; Ghaemi, 2010
379	Frankl, 1978
380	Frankl, 1978, p. 20
381	Giorgi, 2005; Ryback, 2006; Smith, 1978
382	Smith, 1978, p. 31
383	Garrison, 2001, p. 93
384	Bandura, 1982; Bandura & Adams, 1977
385	Bandura, 1996, p. 324
386	DeRobertis, 2013
387	DeRobertis, 2015
388	Beauregard, 2012, p. 3
389	Beauregard, 2012, p. 15
390	Slaby & Gallagher, 2014
391	Slaby & Gallagher, 2014, p. 34
392	Clark, 2001
393	Wilson, 2002, p. 629
394	Clark, 2013
395	Clark, 2013, p. 14
396	Clark, 2013
397	Noë, 2009
398	Noë, 2009, p. 48
399	Dehaen, 2014
400	Dehaene, 2014, p. 11
401	Graham, 2013
402	Carandini, 2015
403	Carandini, 2015, p. 179
404	Yanchar & Hill, 2003, p. 18
405	Dar-Nimrod & Heine, 2011, p. 804
406	Racine, Waldman, Rosenberg, & Illes, 2010, p. 731
407	Keyser & Nagel, 2014, p. 61
408	Noë, 2009, p. xii
409	Baumeister, Masicampo, & DeWall, 2009
410	Vohs & Schooler, 2008
411	Rigoni, Kuhn, Gaudino, Sartori, & Brass, 2012
412	Rigoni, Wilquin, Brass, & Burle, 2013
413	Lynn, Muhle-Karbe, Aarts, & Brass, 2014
414	Lynn, Van Dessel, & Brass, 2013
415	Zhao, Liu, Zhang, Shi, & Huang, 2014
416	Crescioni, Baumeister, Ainsworth, Ent, & Lambert, 2015
417	Rigoni & Brass, 2014, p. 8
418	Raese, 2015
419	Lebowitz, 2014
420	Deng, Luo, Vorperian, Petzold, & Nelson, 2014; Fuchs, 2012; Goldberg, Bell, & Pollard, 2014; Linden, 2014

421   Blease, 2014; McMullen & Sigurdson, 2014; O'Connor, Rees, & Joffe, 2012; Park & Ahn, 2013; Pescosolido et al., 2013

422   Hansell et al., 2011

423   Baker & Proctor, 2013; Buchman, Borgelt, Whiteley, & Illes, 2013; Cohen & Hughes, 2011; France, Lysaker, & Robinson, 2007; Read, Cartwright, Gibson, Shiels, & Magliano, 2015

424   Deacon & Baird, 2009, p. 421

425   Deacon & Baird, 2009, p. 422

426   Deacon & Baird, 2009, p. 429

427   Lebowitz, Ahn, & Nolen-Hoeksema, 2013, p. 521

428   Lebowitz et al., 2013, p. 522

429   Lebowitz et al., 2013, p. 523

430   Lebowitz et al, 2013, p. 525

431   Read, Cartwright, Gibson, Shiels, & Haslam, 2014, p. 237

432   Read, Cartwright, Gibson, Shiels, & Haslam, 2014, p. 240

433   Read, Cartwright, Gibson, Shiels, & Haslam, 2014, p. 240

434   Read, Cartwright, Gibson, Shiels, & Haslam, 2014, p. 240

435   Kemp et al., 2014, p. 48

436   Kemp et al., 2014, p. 48

437   Kemp et al., 2014, p. 50

438   Kemp et al., 2014, p. 50

439   Kemp et al., 2014, p. 50

440   Schroder et al., 2014, p. 121

441   Schroder et al., 2014, p. 121

442   Schroder et al., 2014, p. 124

443   Schroder et al., 2014, p. 127

444   Schroder et al., 2014, p. 129

445   Schroder et al. 2014, p. 130

446   Schroder et al. 2014, p. 134

447   Schroder et al. 2014, p. 135

448   Lebowitz & Ahn, 2014, p. 17787

449   Lebowitz & Ahn, 2014, p. 17787

450   Lebowitz & Ahn, 2014, p. 17788

451   Lebowitz & Ahn, 2014, p. 17788

452   Lebowitz & Ahn, 2014, p. 17788

453   Kvaale et al., 2013; Lam & Salkovskis, 2007; Lebowitz, Pyun, & Ahn, 2014

454   Byrne, Sullivan, & Elsom, 2006; Meyer et al., 2002

455   Blease, 2014

456   Deacon, 2013; Kirsch, 2014a; Schultz, 2015a

☀ Bibliography

All abbreviations conform to those given by the American Psychological Association.

Abbass, A. A., Nowoweiski, S. J., Bernier, D., Tarzwell, R., & Beutel, M. E. (2014). Review of psychodynamic psychotherapy neuroimaging studies. *Psychotherapy and Psychosomatics, 83*, 142-147.

Abramovitch, A. & Schweiger, A. (2015). Misuse of cognitive neuropsychology in psychiatry research: The intoxicating appeal of neo-reductionism. *Behavior Therapist, 38*(7), 184-191.

Akdeniz, C., Tost, H., Streit, F., Haddad, L., Wüst, S., Schäfer, A., . . . Meyer-Lindenberg, A. (2014). Neuroimaging evidence for a role of neural social stress processing in ethnic minority- associated environmental risk. *JAMA Psychiatry, 71*(6), 672-680.

Alladin, A. (2013). The power of belief and expectancy in understanding and management of depression. *American Journal of Clinical Hypnosis, 55*(3), 249-271. doi:10.1080/00029157.2012.740607

Almasi, E. A., Stafford, R. S., Kravitz, R. L., & Mansfield, P. R. (2006). What are the public health effects of direct-to-consumer drug advertising? *PLoS Medicine, 3*(3), e145.

American Diabetes Association. (2014). Diagnosis and classification of diabetes mellitus. *Diabetes Care, 37*, S81.

American Psychiatric Association. (2013). *Diagnostic and statistical manual of mental disorders* (5th ed.). Arlington, VA.

Andreasen, N. C., Liu, D., Ziebell, S., Vora, A., & Ho, B. C. (2013). Relapse duration, treatment intensity, and brain tissue loss in schizophrenia: A prospective longitudinal MRI study. *American Journal of Psychiatry, 170*, 609-615.

Andrews, P. W., Bharwani, A., Lee, K. R., Fox, M., & Thomson, J. A. (2015). Is serotonin an upper or a downer? The evolution of the serotonergic system and its role in depression and the antidepressant response. *Neuroscience & Biobehavioral Reviews, 51*, 164-188. doi:10.1016/j.neubiorev.2015.01.018

Andrews, P. W., Thomson, J. A., Jr., Amstadter, A., & Neale, M. C. (2012). Primum non nocere: An evolutionary analysis of whether antidepressants do more harm than good. *Frontiers in Psychology, 3*, 117.

Angermeyer, M. C., Holzinger, A., Carta, M. G., & Schomerus, G. (2011). Biogenetic explanations and public acceptance of mental illness: Systematic review of population studies. *The British Journal of Psychiatry, 199*(5), 367-372.

Angermeyer, M. C., Millier, A., Kouki, M., Refaï, T., Schomerus, G., & Toumi, M. (2014). Biogenetic explanations and emotional reactions to people with schizophrenia and major depressive disorder. *Psychiatry Research, 220*(1), 702-704.

Arpaly, N. (2005). How it is not "just like diabetes": Mental disorders and the moral psychologist. *Philosophical Issues, 15*(1), 282-298.

Axelrod, J., Whitby, I. G., Hertting, G., & Kopin, I. L. (1961). Studies on the metabolism of catecholamines. *Circulation Research, 9*(3), 715-719. doi:10.1161/01.RES.9.3.715

Axline, V. (1969). *Play therapy* (Rev. ed.). New York, NY: Ballantine.

Baggerly, J. N., Ray, D. C., & Bratton, S. C. (Eds.). (2010). *Child-centered play therapy research: The evidence base for effective practice.* Hoboken, NJ: John Wiley & Sons.

Baker, A. E. Z., & Procter, N. G. (2013). A qualitative inquiry into consumer beliefs about the causes of mental illness. *Journal of Psychiatric and Mental Health Nursing, 20*(5), 442-447. doi:10.1111/jpm.2013.20.issue-5

Ball, J. R. B., & Kiloh, L. G. (1959). A controlled trial of imipramine in treatment of depressive states. *British Medical Journal, 2*(5159), 1052-1055.

Bandura, A. (1996). Ontological and epistemological terrains revisited. *Journal of Behavior Therapy and Experimental Psychiatry, 27*, 323-345.

Bandura, A. (1991). Social cognitive theory of self-regulation. *Organizational Behavior and Human Decision Processes, 50*(2), 248-287.

Bandura, A. (1982). Self-efficacy mechanism in human agency. *American Psychologist, 37*, 122-147.

Bandura, A., & Adams, N. E. (1977). Analysis of self-efficacy theory of behavioral change. *Cognitive Therapy and Research, 1*, 287-310.

Barbui, C., Cipriani, A., & Kirsch, I. (2009). Is the Paroxetine-placebo efficacy separation mediated by adverse events? A systematic re-examination of randomized double-blind studies. Submitted for publication.

Barbui, C., Furukawa, T. A., & Cipriani, A. (2008). Effectiveness of paroxetine in the treatment of acute major depression in adults: A systematic re-examination of published and unpublished data from randomized trials. *Canadian Medical Association Journal, 178*(3), 296-305.

Baumeister, A. A., Hawkins, M. F., & Uzelac, S. M. (2003). The myth of reserpine-induced depression: Role in the historical development of the monoamine theory. *Journal of the History of the Neurosciences, 12*(2), 207-220.

Baumeister, R. F. (2008). Free will in scientific psychology. *Perspectives on Psychological Science, 3*(1), 14-19.

Baumeister, R. F., Masicampo, E. J., & DeWall, C. N. (2009). Prosocial benefits of feeling free: Disbelief in free will increases aggression and reduces helpfulness. *Personality and Social Psychology Bulletin, 35,* 260-268.

Bear, M. F., Connors, B. W., & Paradiso, M. A. (Eds.). (2007). *Neuroscience* (3rd ed.). Baltimore, MD: Lippincott Williams & Wilkins.

Beauregard, M. (2007). Mind does really matter: evidence from neuroimaging studies of emotional self-regulation, psychotherapy, and placebo effect. *Progress in Neurobiology, 81*(4), 218-236.

Beauregard, M. (2012). *Brain wars: The scientific battle over the existence of the mind and the proof that will change the way we live our lives.* New York, NY: HarperCollins.

Beck, A. T. (1963). Thinking and depression: I. Idiosyncratic content and cognitive distortions. Archives of General Psychiatry, 9(4), 324-333.

Beck, A. T., & Alford, B. A. (2009). *Depression: Causes and Treatment.* Philadelphia, PA: University of Pennsylvania Press.

Beck, A. T., & Dozois, D. J. (2011). Cognitive therapy: current status and future directions. *Annual Review of Medicine, 62,* 397-409.

Beck, A. T., Steer, R. A., & Carbin, M. G. (1988). Psychometric properties of the Beck Depression Inventory: Twenty-five years of evaluation. *Clinical Psychology Review, 8*(1), 77-100.

Bennett, M., Dennett, D., Hacker, P., & Searle, J. (2009). *Neuroscience and philosophy: Brain, mind, and language.* New York, NY: Columbia University Press.

Bennett, M. M. & Eberts, S. (2013). Self-expression. In C. E. Schaefer & A. Drewes (Eds.), *The therapeutic powers of play: Core agents of change* (pp. 11-23). New York, NY: John Wiley & Sons.

Bentall, R. (2006). Madness explained: Why we must reject the Kraepelinian paradigm and replace it with a "complaint-orientated" approach to understanding mental illness. *Medical Hypotheses, 66,* 220-233.

Berk, L. E., Mann, T. D., & Ogan, A. T. (2006). Make-believe play: Wellspring for development of self-regulation. In D. Singer, R. Golinkoff, & K. Hirsh-Pasek (Eds.), *Play = learning; How play motivates and enhances children's cognitive and social-emotional growth* (pp. 74-100). Oxford, England: Oxford University Press.

Bharadwaj, P., Pai, M. M., & Suziedelyte, A. (2015). Mental health stigma. *National Bureau of Economic Research, No. w21240,* 1-46). Retrieved from http://economics.ucr.edu/seminars_colloquia/2014-15/applied_economics/Suziedelyte%20paper%20for%206%205%2015%20seminar.pdf

Blanco, P. J., Ray, D. C., & Holliman, R. (2012). Long-term child centered play therapy and academic achievement of children: A follow-up study. *International Journal of Play Therapy, 21*(1), 1-13.

Blease, C. (2014). The duty to be well-informed: The case of depression. *Journal of Medical Ethics, 40,* 225-229.

Bondi, L., & Burman, E. (2001). Women and mental health: A feminist review. *Feminist Review, 68*(1), 6-33.

Borrell-Carrió, F., Suchman, A. L., & Epstein, R. M. (2004). The biopsychosocial model 25 years later: Principles, practice, and scientific inquiry. *Annals of Family Medicine, 2,* 576-582.

Bourgeois, F. T., Kim, J. M., & Mandl, K. D. (2014). Premarket safety and efficacy studies for ADHD medications in children. *PLoS One, 9*(7), retrieved from http://journals.plos.org/plosone/article?id=10.1371/journal.pone.0102249

Bratton, S. C. (2016). The empirical support for play therapy: Strengths and limitations. In K. J. O'Connor, C. E. Schaefer, & L. D. Braverman (Eds.), *Handbook of play therapy* (pp. 651-668). Hoboken, NJ: Wiley.

Bratton, S. C., Ray, D., Rhine, T., & Jones, L. (2005). The efficacy of play therapy with children: A meta-analytic review of treatment outcomes. *Professional Psychology: Research and Practice, 36*(4), 376-390.

Breedlove, S. M., Rosenzweig, M. R., & Watson, N. V. (2007). *Biological psychology: An introduction to behavioral, cognitive, and clinical neuroscience* (5th ed.). Sunderland, MA: Sinauer Associates.

Breggin, P. R. (2001). *The antidepressant fact book: What your doctor won't tell you about Prozac, Zoloft, Paxil, Celexa, and Luvox.* Cambridge, MA: Basic Books.

Bring Change 2 Mind (2016). *The Facts.* Retrieved from http://bringchange2mind.org/learn/the-facts/

British Psychological Society. (2013). *Division of Clinical Psychology position statement on the classification of behaviour and experience in relation to functional psychiatric diagnoses: Time for a paradigm shift.* Leicester, England: British Psychological Society. Retrieved from http://dxrevisionwatch.files.wordpress.com/2013/05/position-statement-on-diagnosis-master-doc.pdf

Brown, R. C., Berenz, E. C., Aggen, S. H., Gardner, C. O., Knudsen, G. P., Reichborn-Kjennerud, T., . . . Amstadter, A. B. (2014). Trauma exposure and Axis I psychopathology: A co-twin control analysis in Norwegian young adults. *Psychological Trauma, 6*(6), 652-660.

Buchman, D. Z., Borgelt, E. L., Whiteley, L., & Illes, J. (2013). Neurobiological narratives: Experiences of mood disorder through the lens of neuroimaging. *Sociology of Health & Illness, 35*(1), 66-81.

Bush, G. (1990). *Presidential Proclamation 6158.* Retrieved from http://www.loc.gov/loc/brain/proclaim.html

Byrne, M. K., Sullivan, N. L., & Elsom, S. J. (2006). Clinician optimism: Development and psychometric analysis of a scale for mental health clinicians. *Australian Journal of Rehabilitation Counselling, 12*(1), 11-20.

Cabaniss, D. L., Moga, D. E., & Oquendo, M. A. (2015). Rethinking the biopsychosocial formulation. *The Lancet Psychiatry, 2*(7), 579-581.

Carandini, M. (2015). From circuits to behavior: A bridge too far? In G. Marcus & J. Freeman (Eds.), *The future of the brain: Essays by the world's leading neuroscientists* (pp. 177-185). Princeton, NJ: Princeton University Press.

Carvalho, A. F., Sharma, M. S., Brunoni, A. R., Vieta, E., & Fava, G. A. (2016). The safety, tolerability and risks associated with the use of newer generation antidepressant drugs: A critical review of the literature. *Psychotherapy and Psychosomatics, 85*(5), 270-288.

Casey, B. J., Craddock, N., Cuthbert, B. N., Hyman, S. E., Lee, F. S., & Ressler, K. J. (2013). DSM-5 and RDoC: Progress in psychiatry research? *Nature Reviews Neuroscience, 14*(11), 810-814.

Chantler, K. (2005). From disconnection to connection: 'Race', gender and the politics of therapy. *British Journal of Guidance & Counselling, 33*(2), 239-256.

Choudhury, S., & Slaby, J. (Eds.). (2011). *Critical neuroscience: A handbook of the social and cultural contexts of neuroscience.* Malden, MA: Blackwell.

Churchland, P. S. (2013). *Touching a nerve: The self as brain.* New York, NY: W.W. Norton.

Clark, A. (2013). Whatever next? Predictive brains, situated agents, and the future of cognitive science. *Behavioral and Brain Sciences, 36*(3), 1-73.

Clark, A. (2001). Reasons, robots and the extended mind. *Mind & Language, 16*, 121-145.

Cohen, J. (1988). *Statistical power analysis for the behavioral sciences* (2nd ed.). Hillsdale, NJ: Lawrence Associates, Publishers.

Cohen, D., & Hughes, S. (2011). How do people taking psychiatric drugs explain their "chemical imbalance?" *Ethical Human Psychology and Psychiatry, 13*(3), 176-189.

Cole, C. E., Patterson, R. M., Craig, J. B., Thomas, W. E., Ristine, L. P., Stahly, M., & Pasamanick, B. (1959). A controlled study of efficacy of iproniazid in treatment of depression. *AMA Archives of General Psychiatry, 1*(5), 513-518.

Cole, E. R. (2009). Intersectionality and research in psychology. *American Psychologist, 64*(3), 170-180.

Coleman, D., Walker, J. S., Lee, J., Friesen, B. J., & Squire, P. N. (2009). Children's beliefs about causes of childhood depression and ADHD: A study of stigmatization. *Psychiatric Services, 60*(7), 950-957.

Constantino, M. J. (2012). Believing is seeing: An evolving research program on patients' psychotherapy expectations. *Psychotherapy Research, 22*(2), 127-138.

Constantino, M. J., Ametrano, R. M., & Greenberg, R. P. (2012). Clinician interventions and participant characteristics that foster adaptive patient expectations for psychotherapy and psychotherapeutic change. *Psychotherapy, 49*(4), 557-569.

Coplan, J. D., Gopinath, S., Abdallah, C. G., & Berry, B. R. (2014). A neurobiological hypothesis of treatment-resistant depression — Mechanisms for selective serotonin reuptake inhibitor non-efficacy. *Frontiers in Behavioral Neuroscience, 8*(189), 1-16.

Coppen, A. (1967). The biochemistry of affective disorders. *British Journal of Psychiatry, 113*, 1237-1264.

Corrigan, P. W. (2000). Mental health stigma as social attribution: Implications for research methods and attitude change. *Clinical Psychology: Science and Practice, 7*(1), 48-67.

Corrigan, P. W., Druss, B. G., & Perlick, D. A. (2014). The impact of mental illness stigma on seeking and participating in mental health care. *Psychological Science in the Public Interest, 15*(2), 37-70.

Corrigan, P. W., River, L. P., Lundin, R. K., Wasowski, K. U., Campion, J., Mathisen, J., . . . Kubiak, M. A. (2000). Stigmatizing attributions about mental illness. *Journal of Community Psychology, 28*(1), 91-102.

Corrigan, P. W., & Watson, A. C. (2004). At issue: Stop the stigma: Call mental illness a brain disease. *Schizophrenia Bulletin, 30*, 477-479.

Cortese, S., Holtmann, M., Banaschewski, T., Buitelaar, J., Coghill, D., Danckaerts, M., . . . Sergeant, J. (2013). Practitioner review: current best practice in the management of adverse events during treatment with ADHD medications in children and adolescents. *Journal of Child Psychology and Psychiatry, 54*(3), 227-46.

Crane, G. E. (1956). The psychiatric side-effects of iproniazid. *The American Journal of Psychiatry, 112*, 494-501.

Crenshaw, D. A. & Kenney-Noziska, S. (2014). Therapeutic presence in play therapy. *International Journal of Play Therapy, 23*(1), 31-43.

Crescioni, A. W., Baumeister, R. F., Ainsworth, S. E., Ent, M., & Lambert, N. M. (2015). Subjective correlates and consequences of belief in free will. *Philosophical Psychology*. Advance online publication. doi:10.1080/095150 89.2014.996285

Cuijpers, P., Berking, M., Andersson, G., Quigley, L., Kleiboer, A., & Dobson, K. S. (2013). A meta-analysis of cognitive-behavioural therapy for adult depression, alone and in comparison with other treatments. *The Canadian Journal of Psychiatry, 58*(7), 376-385.

Cuijpers, P., Sijbrandij, M., Koole, S. L., Andersson, G., Beekman, A. T., & Reynolds, C. F. (2013). The efficacy of psychotherapy and pharmacotherapy in treating depressive and anxiety disorders: a meta-analysis of direct comparisons. *World Psychiatry, 12*(2), 137-148.

Crystal, S., Mackie, T., Fenton, M. C., Amin, S. Neese-Todd, S., Olfson, M., & Bilder, S. (2016). Rapid growth of antipsychotic prescriptions for children who are publicly insured has ceased, but concerns remain. *Health Affairs, 35*(6), 974-982.

Currie, J. (2005). The marketization of depression: The prescribing of SSRI antidepressants to women. *Women and Health Protection*. Retrieved from http://www.naturopath4you.com/PDFs/Depression.pdf

DAFNE Study Group. (2002). "Training in flexible, intensive insulin management to enable dietary freedom in people with type 1 diabetes: dose adjustment for normal eating (DAFNE) randomised controlled trial." *British Medical Journal*, 746-749.

Dar-Nimrod, I., & Heine, S. J. (2011). Genetic essentialism: On the deceptive determinism of DNA. *Psychological Bulletin, 137*, 800-818.

Davies, D. (2010). *A psychiatrist's prescription for his profession*. [Interview]. Retrieved from https://www.npr.org/templates/transcript/transcript. php?storyId=128107547

De Maat, S., Dekker, J., Schoevers, R., & De Jonghe, F. (2006). Relative efficacy of psychotherapy and pharmacotherapy in the treatment of depression: A meta-analysis. *Psychotherapy Research, 16*(5), 566-578.

Deacon, B. J. (2013). The biomedical model of mental disorder: A critical analysis of its validity, utility, and effects on psychotherapy research. *Clinical Psychology Review, 33*(7), 846-861.

Deacon, B. J., & Baird, G. L. (2009). The chemical imbalance explanation of depression: Reducing blame at what cost? *Journal of Social & Clinical Psychology, 28,* 415-435.

Deacon, B. J., & Spielmans, G. I. (in press). Is the efficacy of "antidepressant" medications overrated? In S. O. Lilienfeld & I. D. Waldman (Eds.), *Psychological science under scrutiny: Recent challenges and proposed remedies.* New York, NY: John Wiley and Sons.

Deci, E. L. & Ryan, R. M. (2000). The 'what' and 'why' of goal pursuits: Human needs and the self-determination of behavior. *Psychological Inquiry, 11*(4), 227-268.

Deckersbach, T., Das, S. K., Urban, L. E., Salinardi, T., Batra, P., Rodman, A. M., . . . Roberts, S. B. (2014). Pilot randomized trial demonstrating reversal of obesity-related abnormalities in reward system responsivity to food cues with a behavioral intervention. *Nutrition & Diabetes, 4,* e129. http://dx.doi.org/10.1038/nutd.2014.26

Dehaene, S. (2014). *Consciousness and the brain: Deciphering how the brain codes our thoughts.* New York, NY: Penguin.

Deng, H., Luo, T., Vorperian, S., Petzold, C., & Nelson, D. (2014). Dopamine reuptake inhibition as the means of antidepressant mechanism of function (LB92). *Journal of the Federation of American Societies for Experimental Biology, 28*(1 Suppl.), LB92.

DeRobertis, E. M. (2015). A neuroscientific renaissance of humanistic psychology. *Journal of Humanistic Psychology, 55,* 323-345.

DeRobertis, E. M. (2013). Humanistic psychology alive in the 21st century? *Journal of Humanistic Psychology, 53,* 419-437.

Dorrington, S., Zavos, H., Ball, H., McGuffin, P., Rijsdijk, F., Siribaddana, S., & Hotopf, M. (2014). Trauma, post-traumatic stress disorder and psychiatric disorders in a middle-income setting: Prevalence and comorbidity. *The British Journal of Psychiatry, 205,* 383–389.

Douaud, G., Smith, S., Jenkinson, M., Behrens, T., Johansen-Berg, H., Vickers, J., . . . James, A. (2007). Anatomically related grey and white matter abnormalities in adolescent-onset schizophrenia. *Brain, 130,* 2375–2386.

Dretske, F. (2004). Psychological vs. biological explanations of behavior. *Behavior and Philosophy, 32,* 167-177.

Drewes, A. & Schaefer, C. E. (2013a). Catharsis. In C. E. Schaefer & A. Drewes (Eds.), *The therapeutic powers of play: Core agents of change* (pp. 71-80). New York, NY: John Wiley & Sons.

Drewes, A. & Schaefer, C. E. (2013b). How play therapy causes therapeutic change. In C. E. Schaefer & A. Drewes (Eds.) *The therapeutic powers of play: Core agents of change* (pp. 1-5). New York, NY: John Wiley & Sons.

Durisko, Z., Mulsant, B. H., & Andrews, P. W. (2015). An adaptationist perspective on the etiology of depression. *Journal of Affective Disorders, 172*, 315-323.

Ehrmann, D., Bergis-Jurgan, N., Haak, T., Kulzer, B., & Hermanns, N. (2016). Comparison of the efficacy of a diabetes education programme for type 1 diabetes (PRIMAS) in a randomised controlled trial setting and the effectiveness in a routine care setting: Results of a comparative effectiveness study. *PloS one, 11*(1), e0147581.

Elias, C. & Berk, L. E. (2002). Self-regulation in young children: Is there a role for sociodramatic play? *Early Childhood Research Quarterly, 17*(2), 216-238.

Ellis, A. (1987). A sadly neglected cognitive element in depression. *Cognitive Therapy and Research, 11*(1), 121-145.

Ellis, A. (1962). *Reason and emotion in psychotherapy*. New York, NY: Lyle Stewart.

Eluvathingal, T. J., Chugani, H. T., Behen, M. E., Juhász, C., Muzik, O., Maqbool, M., . . . Makki, M. (2006). Abnormal brain connectivity in children after early severe socioemotional deprivation: A diffusion tensor imaging study. *Pediatrics, 117*(6), 2093-2100.

Epel, E. S., Blackburn, E. H., Lin, J., Dhabhar, F. S., Adler, N. E., Morrow, J. D., & Cawthon, R. (2004). Accelerated telomere shortening in response to life stress. *Proceedings of the National Academy of Sciences of the United States of America, 101*(49), 17312-17315.

Fagen, R. (1981). *Animal play behavior*. New York, NY: Oxford University Press.

Farrell, N. R., Lee, A. A., & Deacon, B. J. (2015). Biological or psychological? Effects of eating disorder psychoeducation on self-blame and recovery expectations among symptomatic individuals. *Behaviour Research and Therapy, 74*, 32-37.

Fava, G. A., Gatti, A., Belaise, C., Guidi, J., & Offidani, E. (2015). Withdrawal symptoms after selective serotonin reuptake inhibitor discontinuation: A systematic review. *Psychotherapy and Psychosomatics, 84*(2), 72-81.

Fedewa, A. L., Ahn, S., Reese, R. J., Suarez, M. M., Macquoid, A., Davis, M. C., & Prout, H. T. (2016). Does psychotherapy work with school-aged youth? A meta-analytic examination of moderator variables that influence therapeutic outcomes. *Journal of School Psychology, 56,* 59-87.

Fisher, K. R., Hirsh-Pasek, K., Newcombe, N., & Golinkoff, R. M. (2013). Taking shape: Supporting preschoolers' acquisition of geometric knowledge through guided play. *Child Development, 81*(6), 1872-1878.

Fodor, J. (1997). Special sciences: Still autonomous after all these years. *Noûs, 31*(s11), 149-163.

Fosgerau, C.F., & Davidsen, A.S. (2014). Patients' perspectives on antidepressant treatment in consultation with physicians. *Qualitative Health Research, 24*(5),641-653.

Fountoulakis, K. N., & Möller, H. J. (2011). Efficacy of antidepressants: A re-analysis and re-interpretation of the Kirsch data. *The International Journal of Neuropsychopharmacology, 14*(03), 405-412.

Fournier, J. C., DeRubeis, R. J., Hollon, S. D., Dimidjian, S., Amsterdam, J. D., Shelton, R. C., & Fawcett, J. (2010). Antidepressant drug effects and depression severity: A patient-level meta-analysis. Journal of the American Medical Association, *303*(1), 47-53.

France, C. M., Lysaker, P. H., & Robinson, R. P. (2007). The "chemical imbalance" explanation for depression: Origins, lay endorsement, and clinical implications. *Professional Psychology: Research and Practice, 38,* 411-420.

Frances, A. (2014). RDoC is necessary, but very oversold. *World Psychiatry, 13*(1), 47-49.

Frankl, V. E. (1980). *The doctor and the soul: From psychotherapy to logotherapy.* New York, NY: Random House.

Frankl, V. E. (1978). *The unheard cry for meaning: Psychotherapy and humanism.* New York, NY: Washington Square Press.

Frazzetto, G., & Anker, S. (2009). Neuroculture. *Nature Reviews Neuroscience, 10,* 815-821.

Fried, E. I. (2015). Problematic assumptions have slowed down depression research: why symptoms, not syndromes are the way forward. *Frontiers in Psychology, 6,* 309, 1-11.

Fried, E. I., van Borkulo, C. D., Epskamp, S., Schoevers, R. A., Tuerlinckx, F., & Borsboom, D. (2016). Measuring depression over time... or not? Lack of unidimensionality and longitudinal measurement invariance in four common rating scales of depression. *Psychological Assessment,* http://psycnet.apa.org/doi/10.1037/pas0000275

Friedberg, R. D., & McClure, J. M. (2015). *Clinical practice of cognitive therapy with children and adolescents: The nuts and bolts.* New York, NY: Guilford Publications.

Freis, E. D. (1954). Mental depression in hypertensive patients treated for long periods with large doses of reserpine. *New England Journal of Medicine, 251*(25), 1006-1008.

Fuchs, T. (2012). Are mental illnesses diseases of the brain? In S. Choudhury & J. Slaby (Eds.), *Critical neuroscience: A handbook of the social and cultural contexts of neuroscience* (pp. 331-344). Oxford, England: Blackwell.

Fuchs, T. (2011). The brain: A mediating organ. *Journal of Consciousness Studies, 18,* 196-221.

Fullagar, S. (2009). Negotiating the neurochemical self: Anti-depressant consumption in women's recovery from depression. *Health, 13*(4), 389-406.

Fullagar, S., & O'Brien, W. (2014). Social recovery and the move beyond deficit models of depression: A feminist analysis of mid-life women's self-care practices. *Social Science & Medicine, 117,* 116-124.

Fulton, B. D., Scheffler, R. M., Hinshaw, S. P., Levine, P., Stone, S., Brown, T. T., & Modrek, S. (2009). National variation of ADHD diagnostic prevalence and medication use: Health care providers and education policies. *Psychiatric Services, 60*(80), 1075-1083.

Gammell, D. J., & Stoppard, J. M. (1999). Women's experiences of treatment of depression: Medicalization or empowerment? *Canadian Psychology, 40*(2), 112-128.

Garrison, A. (2001). Restoring the human in humanistic psychology. *Journal of Humanistic Psychology, 41,* 91-104.

Gartlehner, G., Gaynes, B. N., Amick, H. R., Asher, G., Morgan, L. C., Coker-Schwimmer, E., ... & Bann, C. (2015). Nonpharmacological versus pharmacological treatments for adult patients with major depressive disorder. *Comparative Effectiveness Review, 161,*

Gaskill, R. L. & Perry, B. D. (2014). The neurobiological power of play: Using the neurosequential model of therapeutics to guide play in the healing process. In C. Malchiodi & D. Crenshaw (Eds.) *Creative arts and play therapy for attachment problems* (pp. 178-194). New York, NY: Guilford Press.

Ghaemi, S. N. (2013). Taking disease seriously in DSM. *World Psychiatry, 12,* 210-212.

Ghaemi, S. N. (2010). *The rise and fall of the biopsychosocial model: Reconciling art and science in psychiatry.* Baltimore, MD: Johns Hopkins University Press.

Gibson, K., Cartwright, C., & Read, J. (2016). 'In my life antidepressants have been...': a qualitative analysis of users' diverse experiences with antidepressants. *BMC Psychiatry, 16*(1), 1, 1-7.

Gil, E. (1991). *The healing power of play: Working with abused children.* New York, NY: Guilford Press.

Giorgi, A. (2005). Remaining challenges for humanistic psychology. *Journal of Humanistic Psychology, 45,* 204-216.

Godfrey, K. M., Gallo, L. C., & Afari, N. (2015). Mindfulness-based interventions for binge eating: a systematic review and meta-analysis. *Journal of Behavioral Medicine, 38*(2), 348-362.

Gogtay, N. (2008). Cortical brain development in schizophrenia: Insights from neuroimaging studies in childhood-onset schizophrenia. *Schizophrenia Bulletin, 34*(1), 30-36.

Gogtay, N., & Rapoport, J. L. (2008). Childhood-onset schizophrenia: Insights from neuroimaging studies. *Journal of the American Academy of Child and Adolescent Psychiatry, 47*(10), 1120-1124.

Gold, I., & Stoljar, D. (1999). A neuron doctrine in the philosophy of neuroscience. *Behavioral and Brain Sciences, 22,* 809-830.

Goldberg, J. S., Bell, Jr, C. E., & Pollard, D. A. (2014). Revisiting the monoamine theory of depression: A new perspective. *Perspectives in Medicinal Chemistry, 6*, 1-8.

Graham, G. (2013). *The disordered mind: An introduction to philosophy of mind and mental illness.* New York, NY: Routledge.

Gratten, J., Wray, N. R., Keller, M. C., & Visscher, P. M. (2014). Large-scale genomics unveils the genetic architecture of psychiatric disorders. *Nature Neuroscience, 17*(6), 782-790.

Gruen, A. (1998). Reductionistic biological thinking and the denial of experience and pain in developmental theories. *Journal of Humanistic Psychology, 38*, 84-102.

Hamilton, M. (1960). A rating scale for depression. *Journal of Neurology, Neurosurgery & Psychiatry, 23*(1), 56-62.

Hankin, B. J., & Abramson, L. Y. (2001). Development of gender differences in depression: An elaborated cognitive vulnerability-transactional stress theory. *Psychological Bulletin, 127*(6), 773-796.

Hansell, J., Bailin, A. P., Franke, K. A., Kraft, J. M., Wu, H. Y., Dolsen, M. R., . . . Kazi, N. F. (2011). Conceptually sound thinking about depression: An Internet survey and its implications. *Professional Psychology: Research and Practice, 42*, 382-390.

Harris, G. (2009, October 21). Drug makers are advocacy group's biggest donors [Electronic version]. *New York Times.* Retrieved from http://www.nytimes.com/2009/10/22/health/22nami.html?r1

Harrow, M., Jobe, T. H., & Faull, R. N. (2012). Do all schizophrenia patients need antipsychotic treatment continuously throughout their lifetime? A 20-year longitudinal study. *Psychological Medicine, 42*(10), 2145-2155.

Haslam, N. (2011). Genetic essentialism, neuroessentialism, and stigma: Commentary on Dar-Nimrod and Heine (2011). *Psychological Bulletin, 137*, 819-824.

Haslam, N. & Kvaale, E. P. (2015). Biogenetic explanations of mental disorder: The mixed-blessings model. *Current Directions in Psychological Science, 24*(5), 399-404.

Hatala, A. R. (2012). The status of the "biopsychosocial" model in health psychology: Towards an integrated approach and a critique of cultural conceptions. *Open Journal of Medical Psychology, 1*(04), 51-62.

Healy, D. (1997). *The antidepressant era.* Cambridge, MA: Harvard University Press.

Healy, D. (2015). Serotonin and depression. *British Medical Journal, 350*(h1771), 1-2.

Healy, D., & Savage, M. (1998). Reserpine exhumed. *The British Journal of Psychiatry, 172,* 376-378.

Henningsen, P. (2015). Still modern? Developing the biopsychosocial model for the 21st century. *Journal of Psychosomatic Research, 79*(5), 362-363.

Henwood, K., & Pidgeon, N. (1995). Remaking the link: Qualitative research and feminist standpoint theory. *Feminism & Psychology, 5,* 7-30.

Herculano-Houzel, S. (2009). The human brain in numbers: A linearly scaled-up primate brain. *Frontiers in Human Neuroscience, 3,* 31.

Heyman, G. M. (2009). *Addiction: A disorder of choice.* Cambridge, MA: Harvard University Press.

Hilbert, A., Bishop, M. E., Stein, R. I., Tanofsky-Kraff, M., Swenson, A. K., Welch, R. R., & Wilfley, D. E. (2012). Long-term efficacy of psychological treatments for binge eating disorder. *The British Journal of Psychiatry, 200*(3), 232-237.

Holmes, L. (2016). Lena Dunham shuts down mental illness stereotypes in new photos. Retrieved from http://www.huffingtonpost.com/entry/lena-dunham-mental-illness-instagram_us_56a259b7e4b0d8cc1099cf59

Hölzel, B. K., Carmody, J., Vangel, M., Congleton, C., Yerramsetti, S. M., Gard, T., & Lazar, S. W. (2010). Mindfulness practice leads to increases in regional brain gray matter density. *Psychiatry Research, 191,* 36-43.

Horney, K. (1967/1993). *Feminine Psychology.* New York, NY: W. W. Norton & Company.

Horst, S. (2012). *Beyond reduction: Philosophy of mind and post-reductionist philosophy of science.* New York, NY: Oxford University Press.

Horst, S. (2014). *Laws and freedom: A BIT of laws, mind, and free will.* Cambridge, MA: MIT Press.

Howell, B. R., McCormack, K. M., Grand, A. P., Sawyer, N. T., Zhang, X., Maestripieri, D., . . . Sanchez, M. M. (2013). Brain white matter microstructure alterations in adolescent rhesus monkeys exposed to early life stress: Associations with high cortisol during infancy. *Biology of Mood & Anxiety Disorders, 3,* 21. http://dx.doi.org/10.1186/2045-5380-3-21.

Huedo-Medina, T. B., Johnson, B. T., & Kirsch, I. (2012). Kirsch et al.'s (2008) calculations are correct: Reconsidering Fountoulakis & Möller's re-analysis of the Kirsch data. *The International Journal of Neuropsychopharmacology, 15*(8), 1193-1198.

Huizinga, J. (1950). *Homo ludens: A study of the play-element in culture.* New York, NY: Routledge.

Hunter, N., & Schultz, W. (2016). Brain scan research. *Ethical Human Psychology and Psychiatry, 18*(1), In press.

Hurst, S. A., & Genest, M. (1995). Cognitive-behavioural therapy with a feminist orientation: A perspective for therapy with depressed women. *Canadian Psychology, 36*(3), 236-257.

Huxley, A. (1932). *Brave new world.* New York, NY: Harper.

Hyman, S. E. (2010). The diagnosis of mental disorders: The problem of reification. *Annual Review of Clinical Psychology, 6,* 155-179.

Hyman, S. E. (2012). Revolution stalled. *Science Translational Medicine, 4*(155), 155cm11-155cm11.

Hyman, S., & Nestler, E. J. (1996). Initiation and adaptation: A paradigm for understanding psychotropic drug action. *American Journal of Psychiatry, 153,* 151-162.

Insel, T. (2013). *Director's blog: Transforming diagnosis.* Retrieved from http://www.nimh.nih.gov/ about/director/2013/transforming-diagnosis.shtml

Insel, T. (2014). The NIMH Research Domain Criteria (RDoC) Project: Precision medicine for psychiatry. *American Journal of Psychiatry, 171*(4), 395-397.

Insel, T. (2015). A different way of thinking. *New Scientist, 227*(3035), 5.

Insel, T., Cuthbert, B., Garvey, M., Heinssen, R., Pine, D. S., Quinn, K., ... Wang, P. (2010). Research Domain Criteria (RDoC): Toward a new classification framework for research on mental disorders. *American Journal of Psychiatry, 167*(7), 748-751.

International Society for Ethical Psychology and Psychiatry. (2013). *Statement supporting the British Psychological Society's statement on functional psychiatric diagnoses.* Retrieved from http:// psychintegrity. org/wp-content/uploads/2015/08/Supporting-the-British-Psychological-Society%E2%80%99s-Statement-on-Functional-Psychiatric-Diagnoses-May-16-2013.pdf

Ioannidis, J. P. (2008). Effectiveness of antidepressants: An evidence myth constructed from a thousand randomized trials? *Philosophy, Ethics, and Humanities in Medicine, 3*(1), 14.

Iselin, M. G., & Addis, M. E. (2003). Effects of etiology on perceived helpfulness of treatments for depression. *Cognitive Therapy and Research, 27*(2), 205-222.

Janssen, I., Prebendal, L., Bak, M., Hanssen, M., Vollebergh, W., De Graaf, R., & van Os, J. (2004). Childhood abuse as a risk factor for psychotic experiences. *Acta Psychiatrica Scandinavica, 109*(1), 38-45.

Jenkins, E. K. (2014). The politics of knowledge: Implications for understanding and addressing mental health and illness. *Nursing Inquiry, 21*(1), 3-10.

Johnson, B. T., & Kirsch, I. (2008). Do antidepressants work? Statistical significance versus clinical benefits. *Significance, 5*(2), 54-58.

Johnston, C., Seipp, C., Hommersen, P., Hoza, B., & Fine, S. (2005). Treatment choices and experiences in attention deficit and hyperactivity disorder: Relations to parents' beliefs and attributions. *Child: Care, Health and Development, 31*(6), 669-677.

Joseph, J. (2014). *The Trouble with Twin Studies: A Reassessment of Twin Research in the Social and Behavioral Sciences.* New York, NY: Routledge.

Kandel, E. R. (2007). *In search of memory: The emergence of a new science of mind.* New York, NY: W.W. Norton.

Kass, I., & Brown, E. C. (1955). Treatment of hypertensive patients with Rauwolfia compounds and reserpine: Depressive and psychotic changes. *Journal of the American Medical Association, 159*(16), 1513-1516.

Kemp, J. J., Lickel, J. J., & Deacon, B. J. (2014). Effects of a chemical imbalance causal explanation on individuals' perceptions of their depressive symptoms. *Behaviour Research and Therapy, 56*, 47-52.

Kendler, K. S. (2005). Toward a philosophical structure for psychiatry. *The American Journal of Psychiatry, 162*(3), 433-440.

Kessler, R. C., & Bromet, E. J. (2013). The epidemiology of depression across cultures. *Annual Review of Public Health, 34,* 119-138.

Keyser, J., & Nagel, S. K. (2014). Stimulating more than the patient's brain: Deep brain stimulation from a systems perspective. *AJOB Neuroscience, 5*(4), 60-62.

Khalsa, S. R., McCarthy, K. S., Sharpless, B. A., Barrett, M. S., & Barber, J. P. (2011). Beliefs about the causes of depression and treatment preferences. *Journal of Clinical Psychology, 67*(6), 539-549.

Khan, A., Faucett, J., Lichtenberg, P., Kirsch, I., & Brown, W. A. (2012). A systematic review of comparative efficacy of treatments and controls for depression. *PLoS One, 7*(7), e41778.

Khandaker, G. M., Cousins, L., Deakin, J., Lennox, B. R., Yolken, R., & Jones, P. B. (2015). Inflammation and immunity in schizophrenia: Implications for pathophysiology and treatment. *The Lancet, 2*(3), 258-270.

Khin, N. A., Chen, Y. F., Yang, Y., Yang, P., & Laughren, T. P. (2011). Exploratory analyses of efficacy data from major depressive disorder trials submitted to the US food and drug administration in support of new drug applications. *The Journal of Clinical Psychiatry, 72*(4), 464-472.

Kichuk, S. A., Lebowitz, M. S., & Adams, T. G. (2015). Can biomedical models of psychopathology interfere with cognitive-behavioral treatment processes? *The Behavior Therapist, 38*(7), 181-186.

Kielholz, P., & Battegay, R. (1958). Treatment of depressive condition images, with special consideration of Tofranil, a new antidepressant. *Swiss Medical Weekly, 88*(31), 763-767.

Kirsch, I. (1985). Response expectancy as a determinant of experience and behavior. *American Psychologist, 40*(11), 1189-1202.

Kirsch, I. (1997a). Response expectancy theory and application: A decennial review. *Applied & Preventive Psychology, 6*(2), 69-79.

Kirsch, I. (1997b). Specifying nonspecifics: Psychological mechanisms of placebo effects. In A. Harrington (Ed.), *The placebo effect: An interdisciplinary exploration* (pp. 166-186). Cambridge, MA: Harvard University Press.

Kirsch, I. (1999). *How expectancies shape experience*. Washington, DC: American Psychological Association.

Kirsch, I. (2008). Challenging received wisdom: Antidepressants and the placebo effect. *McGill Journal of Medicine, 11*(2), 219.

Kirsch, I. (2010). *The emperor's new drugs: Exploding the antidepressant myth*. New York, NY: Basic Books.

Kirsch, I. (2014a). Antidepressants and the placebo effect. *Zeitschrift für Psychologie, 222*, 128-134.

Kirsch, I. (2014b). The emperor's new drugs: Medication and placebo in the treatment of depression. *Handbook of Experimental Pharmacology, 225*, 291-303.

Kirsch, I., Deacon, B. J., Huedo-Medina, T. B., Scoboria, A., Moore, T. J., & Johnson, B. T. (2008). Initial severity and antidepressant benefits: A meta-analysis of data submitted to the food and drug administration. *PLoS Medicine, 5*(2), e45.

Kirsch, I., & Moncrieff, J. (2007). Clinical trials and the response rate illusion. *Contemporary Clinical Trials, 28*(4), 348-351.

Kirsch, I., Moore, T. J., Scoboria, A., & Nicholls, S. S. (2002). The emperor's new drugs: An analysis of antidepressant medication data submitted to the US food and drug administration. *Prevention & Treatment, 5*(1), 23a.

Kirsch, I., & Sapirstein, G. (1998). Listening to Prozac but hearing placebo: A meta-analysis of antidepressant medication. *Prevention & Treatment, 1*(2), 2a.

Klein, D. F. (1998). Reply to Kirsch's rejoinder regarding antidepressant meta-analysis. *Prevention & Treatment, 1*(2), 8r.

Konofal, E., Lecendreux, M., & Cortese, S. (2010). Sleep and ADHD. *Sleep Medicine, 11*(7), 652-658.

Korpela, K., Kyttä, M., & Hartig, T. (2002). Restorative experience, self-regulation, and children's place preferences. *Journal of Environmental Psychology, 22*(4), 387-398.

Kristeller, J., Wolever, R. Q., & Sheets, V. (2014). Mindfulness-based eating awareness training (MB-EAT) for binge eating: A randomized clinical trial. *Mindfulness, 5*(3), 282-297.

Kuhn, R. (1958). The treatment of depressive states with G 22355 (imipramine hydrochloride). *American Journal of Psychiatry, 115*(5), 459-464.

Kupfer, D. (2013). *News release: Chair of DSM-5 task force discusses future of mental health research.* Arlington, VA: American Psychiatric Association. Retrieved from http://www.psychiatry.org

Kuppin, S., & Carpiano, R. M. (2008). Public conceptions of serious mental illness and substance abuse, their causes and treatments: Findings from the 1996 General Social Survey. *American Journal of Public Health, 98*(1), S120-S125.

Kvaale, E. P., Gottdiener, W. H., & Haslam, N. (2013). Biogenetic explanations and stigma: A meta-analytic review of associations among laypeople. *Social Science & Medicine, 96,* 95-103

Kvaale, E. P., Haslam, N., & Gottdiener, W. H. (2013). The 'side effects' of medicalization: A meta-analytic review of how biogenetic explanations affect stigma. *Clinical Psychology Review, 33,* 782-794.

Labonté, B., Superman, M., Maussion, G., Navaro, L., Yerko, V., Mahar, I., . . . Turecki, G. (2012). Genome-wide epigenetic regulation by early-life trauma. *Archives of General Psychiatry, 69,* 722-731.

Lacasse, J. R., & Leo, J. (2005). Serotonin and depression: A disconnect between the advertisements and the scientific literature. *PLoS Medicine, 2*(12), e392.

Lacasse, J. R., & Leo, J. (2015). Antidepressants and the chemical imbalance theory of depression: A reflection and update on the discourse. *The Behavior Therapist, 38*(7), 206-213.

LaFrance, M. N. (2009). *Women and depression: Recovery and resistance.* London, UK/New York, NY: Routledge.

LaFrance, M. N. (2007). A bitter pill: a discursive analysis of women's medicalized accounts of depression. *Journal of Health Psychology, 12*(1), 127-140.

Lafrance, M. N., & McKenzie-Mohr, S. (2013). The DSM and its lure of legitimacy. *Feminism & Psychology, 23*(1), 119-140.

Lam, D. C., & Salkovskis, P. M. (2007). An experimental investigation of the impact of biological and psychological causal explanations on anxious and depressed patients' perception of a person with panic disorder. *Behaviour Research and Therapy, 45,* 405-411.

Längle, A., & Sykes, B. M. (2006). Viktor Frankl—advocate for humanity: On his 100th birthday. *Journal of Humanistic Psychology, 46*, 36-47.

Leblanc, M. & Ritchie, M. (2001). A meta-analysis of play therapy outcomes. *Counselling Psychology Quarterly, 14*(2), 149-163.

Lebowitz, M. S. (2014). Biological conceptualizations of mental disorders among affected individuals: A review of correlates and consequences. *Clinical Psychology: Science and Practice, 21*(1), 67-83.

Lebowitz, M. S., & Ahn, W. K. (2015). Emphasizing Malleability in the biology of depression: Durable effects on perceived agency and prognostic pessimism. *Behaviour Research and Therapy, 71*, 125-130.

Lebowitz, M. S., & Ahn, W. K. (2014). Effects of biological explanations for mental disorders on clinicians' empathy. *Proceedings of the National Academy of Sciences of the United States of America, 111*(50), 17786-17790.

Lebowitz, M. S., Ahn, W. K., & Nolen-Hoeksema, S. (2013). Fixable or fate? Perceptions of the biology of depression. *Journal of Consulting and Clinical Psychology, 81*(3), 518-527.

Lebowitz, M. S., Pyun, J. J., & Ahn, W. K. (2014). Biological explanations of generalized anxiety disorder: Effects on beliefs about prognosis and responsibility. *Psychiatric Services, 65*, 498-503.

Lee, A. A., Farrell, N. R., McKibbin, C. L., & Deacon, B. J. (2016). Comparing treatment relevant etiological explanations for depression and social anxiety: Effects on self-stigmatizing attitudes. *Journal of Social and Clinical Psychology, 35*(7), 571-588.

Lemieux, G., Davignon, A., & Genest, J. (1956). Depressive states during Rauwolfia therapy for arterial hypertension: A report of 30 cases. *Canadian Medical Association Journal, 74*(7), 522-526.

Leo, J., & Lacasse, J. R. (2008). The media and the chemical imbalance theory of depression. *Society, 45*(1), 35-45.

Leshner, A. I. (1997). Addiction is a brain disease, and it matters. *Science, 278*(5335), 45-47.

Leucht, S., Fennema, H., Engel, R., Kaspers-Janssen, M., Lepping, P., & Szegedi, A. (2013). What does the HAMD mean? *Journal of Affective Disorders, 148*(2), 243-248.

Levin, J. (2013). Functionalism. In *Stanford Encyclopedia of Philosophy*. Retrieved from http://plato.stanford.edu/archives/fall2013/entries/functionalism/

Levy, N. (2013). Addiction is not a brain disease (and it matters). *Frontiers in Psychiatry, 4*, 24.

Lilienfeld, S. O. (2014). The Research Domain Criteria (RDoC): An analysis of methodological and conceptual challenges. *Behaviour Research and Therapy, 62*, 129-139.

Lilienfeld, S. O., & Treadway, M. T. (2016). Clashing diagnostic approaches: DSM-ICD versus RDoC. *Annual Review of Clinical Psychology, 12*, 435-463.

Lillard, A. S. (2015). The development of play. In R. M. Lerner, L.S. Liben, & U. Mueller (Eds.), *Handbook of child psychology and developmental science, cognitive processes* (pp. 425-468). New York, NY: Wiley & Sons.

Lin, Y. & Bratton, S. C. (2015). A meta-analytic review of child-centered play therapy approaches. *Journal of Counseling & Development, 93*(1), 45-58.

Linden, D. E. (2014). Neurofeedback and networks of depression. *Dialogues in Clinical Neuroscience, 16*(1), 103.

Linsey, E. W. & Colwell, M. J. (2003). Preschoolers' emotional competence: Links to pretend and physical play. *Child Study Journal, 33*(1), 39-53.

Loomer, H. P., Saunders, J. C., & Kline, N. S. (1957). A clinical and pharmacodynamic evaluation of iproniazid as a psychic energizer. *Psychiatric Research Reports, 8*, 129-141.

Lynn, M. T., Muhle-Karbe, P. S., Aarts, H., & Brass, M. (2014). Priming determinist beliefs diminishes implicit (but not explicit) components of self-agency. *Frontiers in Psychology, 5*, 1483.

Lynn, M. T., Van Dessel, P., & Brass, M. (2013). The influence of high-level beliefs on self-regulatory engagement: Evidence from thermal pain stimulation. *Frontiers in Psychology, 4*, 614.

MacKay, J. M., & Rutherford, A. (2012). Feminist women's accounts of depression. *Affilia, 27*(2), 180-189.

MacKenzie, L. E., Abidi, S., Fisher, H. L., Propper, L., Bagnell, A., Morash-Conway, J., . . . Uher, R. (2016). Stimulant medication and psychotic symptoms in offspring of parents with mental illness. *Pediatrics, 137*(1), 1-10.

Mann, A. M., & MacPherson, A. S. (1959). Clinical experience with imipramine (G22355) in the treatment of depression. *Canadian Psychiatric Association Journal, 4*(1), 38-47.

Månsson, K. N., Salami, A., Frick, A., Carlbring, P., Andersson, G., Furmark, T., & Boraxbekk, C. J. (2016). Neuroplasticity in response to cognitive behavior therapy for social anxiety disorder. *Translational Psychiatry, 6,* e727, 1-8.

Margraf, J., & Schneider, S. (2016). From neuroleptics to neuroscience and from Pavlov to psychotherapy: more than just the "emperor's new treatments" for mental illnesses?. *EMBO Molecular Medicine,* e201606650.

Marsh, J. K., & Romano, A. L. (2016). Lay judgments of mental health treatment options: The mind versus body problem. *MDM Policy & Practice, 1*(1), 2381468316669361.

McInerney, M., Mellor, J. M., & Nicholas, L. H. (2013). Recession depression: Mental health effects of the 2008 stock market crash. *Journal of Health Economics, 32,* 1090-1104.

McLaren, N. (1998). A critical review of the biopsychosocial model. *Australasian Psychiatry, 32*(1), 86-92.

McLaren, N. (2008). Kandel's "New science of mind" for psychiatry and the limits to reductionism: A critical review. *Ethical Human Psychology and Psychiatry, 10*(2), 109-121.

McMullen, L. M., & Sigurdson, K. J. (2014). Depression is to diabetes as antidepressants are to insulin: The unraveling of an analogy? *Health Communication, 29*(3), 309-317.

Melander, H., Ahlqvist-Rastad, J., Meijer, G., & Beermann, B. (2003). Evidence b(i)ased medicine—Selective reporting from studies sponsored by pharmaceutical industry: Review of studies in new drug applications. *BMJ, 326*(7400), 1171-1173.

Mendels, J., & Frazer, A. (1974). Brain biogenic anime depletion and mood. *Archives of General Psychiatry, 30*(4), 447-451.

Meyer, B., Pilkonis, P. A., Krupnick, J. L., Egan, M. K., Simmens, S. J., & Sotsky, S. M. (2002). Treatment expectancies, patient alliance and outcome: Further analyses from the National Institute of Mental Health Treatment of Depression Collaborative Research Program. *Journal of Consulting and Clinical Psychology, 70,* 1051-1055.

Michael, R. B., Garry, M., & Kirsch, I. (2012). Suggestion, cognition, and behavior. *Current Directions in Psychological Science, 21,* 151-156.

Miller, G. A. (2010). Mistreating psychology in the decades of the brain. *Perspectives on Psychological Science, 5*(6), 716-743.

Moncrieff, J. (2016). Misrepresenting harms in antidepressant trials. *BMJ, 352,* i217.

Moncrieff, J. (2013a). *The bitterest pills: The troubling story of antipsychotic drugs.* New York, NY: Palgrave Macmillan.

Moncrieff, J. (2013b). *Continuing the antidepressant debate: The clinical (ir) relevance of drug-placebo differences.* Retrieved from http://joannamoncrieff. com/2014/07/02/continuing-the-antidepressantdebate-the-clinical-relevance-of-drug-placebo-differences/

Moncrieff, J. (2008). *The myth of the chemical cure: A critique of psychiatric drug treatment.* New York, NY: Palgrave Macmillan.

Moncrieff, J., & Kirsch, I. (2015). Empirically derived criteria cast doubt on the clinical significance of antidepressant-placebo differences. *Contemporary Clinical Trials, 43,* 60-62.

Moncrieff, J., & Kirsch, I. (2005). Efficacy of antidepressants in adults. *British Medical Journal, 331*(7509), 155-157.

Moncrieff, J., Wessely, S., & Hardy, R. (2004). Active placebos versus antidepressants for depression. *Cochrane Database of Systematic Reviews, 1,* 1-27.

Mondloch, M. V., Cole, D. C., & Frank, J. W. (2001). Does how you do depend on how you think you'll do? A systematic review of the evidence for a relation between patients' recovery expectations and health outcomes. *Canadian Medical Association Journal, 165,* 174-179.

Monroe, S. M., & Anderson, S. F. (2015). Depression: The shroud of heterogeneity. *Current Directions in Psychological Science, 24*(3), 227-231.

Moore, M. T., & Fresco, D. M. (2012). Depressive realism: A meta-analytic review. *Clinical Psychology Review, 32,* 496-509.

Mowbray, C. T., Herman, S. E., & Hazel, K. L. (1992). Gender and serious mental illness: A feminist perspective. *Psychology of Women Quarterly, 16,* 107-126.

Mulinari, S. (2012). Monoamine theories of depression: Historical impact on biomedical research. *Journal of the History of the Neurosciences, 21*(4), 366-392.

Müller, U., Fletcher, P. C., & Steinberg, H. (2006). The origin of pharmacopsychology: Emil Kraepelin's experiments in Leipzig, Dorpat and Heidelberg (1882-1892). *Psychopharmacology, 184*, 131-138.

Nabeshima, T., & Kim, H.-C. (2013). Involvement of genetic and environmental factors in the onset of depression. *Experimental Neurobiology, 22*(4), 235-243.

Neville, H. J., Stevens, C., Pakulak, E., Bell, T. A., Fanning, J., Klein, S., & Isbell, E. (2013). Family-based training program improves brain function, cognition, and behavior in lower socioeconomic status preschoolers. *Proceedings of the National Academy of Sciences of the United States of America, 110*(29), 12138-12143.

Newton, E. & Jenvey, V. (2011). Play and theory of mind: Associations with social competence in young children. *Early Child Development and Care, 181*(6), 761-773.

Nicolopoulou, A. (2010). The alarming disappearance of play from early childhood education. *Human Development, 53*(1), 1-4.

Niehoff, D. L., Palacios, J. M., & Kuhar, M. J. (1979). In vivo receptor binding: Attempts to improve specific/non-specific ratios. *Life Sciences, 25*, 819-826.

Nielsen, M., Hansen, E., & Gøtzsche, P. C. (2012). What is the difference between dependence and withdrawal reactions? A comparison of benzodiazepines and selective serotonin reuptake inhibitors. *Addiction, 107*, 900-908.

Noë, A. (2009). *Out of our heads: Why you are not your brain, and other lessons from the biology of consciousness*. New York, NY: Hill & Wang.

Noordermeer, S., Luman, M., & Oosterlaan, J. (2016). A systematic review and meta-analysis of neuroimaging in oppositional defiant disorder (ODD) and conduct disorder (CD) taking attention-deficit hyperactivity disorder (ADHD) in account. *Neuropsychology Review, 26*(1), 44-72.

Obama, B. H. (2013). *Remarks by the president on the BRAIN initiative and innovation*. Retrieved from https://obamawhitehouse.archives.gov/the-press-office/2013/04/02/remarks-president-brain-initiative-and-american-innovation

Obama, M. (2015, March). *Remarks by the First Lady at "Change Direction" mental health event.* Speech presented at the Newseum, Washington, D.C.

O'Brien, W. (2012). The recovery imperative: A critical examination of mid-life women's recovery from depression. *Social Science & Medicine, 75*(3), 573-580.

O'Connor, C., Rees, G., & Joffe, H. (2012). Neuroscience in the public sphere. *Neuron, 74,* 220-226.

O'Connor, K. J. (2000). *The play therapy primer.* Hoboken, NJ: John Wiley & Sons.

Ogawa, Y. (2004). Childhood trauma and play therapy intervention for traumatized children. *Journal of Professional Counselling, Practice, Theory, & Research, 32*(1), 19-29.

Olfson, M., & Marcus, S. C. (2009). National patterns in antidepressant medication treatment. *Archives of General Psychiatry, 66*(8), 848-856.

Papakostas, G. I., Shelton, R. C., Kinrys, G., Henry, M. E., Bakow, B. R., Lipkin, S. H., . . . Bilello, J. A. (2013). Assessment of a multi-assay, serum-based biological diagnostic test for major depressive disorder: A pilot and replication study. *Molecular Psychiatry, 18,* 332-339.

Paris, J. & Kirmayer, L. J. (2016). The National Institute of Mental Health Research Domain Criteria: A bridge too far. *The Journal of Nervous and Mental Disease, 204*(1), 26-32.

Park, J., & Ahn, H. (2013). Direct-to-consumer (DTC) antidepressant advertising and consumer misperceptions about the chemical imbalance theory of depression: The moderating role of skepticism. *Health Marketing Quarterly, 30*(4), 362-378.

Park, J. S., & Grow, J. M. (2008). The social reality of depression: DTC advertising of antidepressants and perceptions of the prevalence and lifetime risk of depression. *Journal of Business Ethics, 79,* 379-393

Parrott, R. (2004). Emphasizing "communication" in health communication. *Journal of Communication, 54*(4), 751-787.

Pelham, Jr., W. E. & Fabiano, G. (2008). Evidence-based psychosocial treatments for attention-deficit/hyperactivity disorder. *Journal of Clinical Child & Adolescent Psychology, 37*(1), 184-214.

Pelham, Jr., W. E., Gnagy, E. M., Greiner, A. R., Hoza, B., Hinshaw, S. P., Swanson, J. M., . . . McBurnett, K. (2000). Behavioral versus behavioral and pharmacological treatment in ADHD children attending a summer treatment program. *Journal of Abnormal Child Psychology, 28*(6), 507-525.

Pellegrini, A. D. & Smith, P. K. (1998). The development of play during childhood: Forms and possible functions. *Child Psychology and Psychiatry Review, 3*(2), 51-57.

Penfold, S., & Walker, G. (1984). *Women and the psychiatric paradox.* Maidenhead, England: Open University Press.

Pescosolido, B. A., Martin, J. K., Long, J. S., Medina, T. R., Phelan, J. C., & Link, B. G. (2010). "A disease like any other"? A decade of change in public reactions to schizophrenia, depression, and alcohol dependence. *American Journal of Psychiatry, 167*(11), 1321-1330.

Phillips, M. R. (2014), Will RDoC hasten the decline of America's global leadership role in mental health? *World Psychiatry, 13*(1), 40-41.

Pies, R. (2011). Psychiatry's new brain-mind and the legend of the chemical imbalance. *Psychiatric Times, 11,* 1.

Pies, R. (2014). Nuances, narratives, and the "chemical imbalance" debate. *Psychiatric Times, 31*(4), 5-6.

Pincus, H. A., Tanielian, T. L., Marcus, S. C., Olfson, M., Zarin, D. A., Thompson, J., & Zito, J. M. (1998). Prescribing trends in psychotropic medications: Primary care, psychiatry, and other medical specialties. *Journal of the American Medical Association, 279,* 526-531.

Place, U. T. (1956). Is consciousness a brain process? *British Journal of Psychology, 47*(1), 44-50.

Platt, R., & Sears, H. T. N. (1956). Reserpine in severe hypertension. *The Lancet, 267*(6920), 401-403.

Pratt, L. A., Brody, D. J., & Gu, Q. (2011). *Antidepressant use in persons aged 12 and over: United States, 2005-2008* (NCHS Data Brief No. 76). Atlanta, GA: Centers for Disease Control and Prevention.

Putnam, H. (1980). The nature of mental states. *Readings in Philosophy of Psychology, 1,* 223-231.

Rabkin, J. G., Markowitz, J. S., Stewart, J., McGrath, P., Harrison, W., Quitkin, F. M., & Klein, D. F. (1986). How blind is blind? Assessment of patient and doctor medication guesses in a placebo-controlled trial of imipramine and phenelzine. *Psychiatry Research, 19*(1), 75-86.

Racine, E. (2015). Neuroscience, neuroethics, and the media. *Handbook of Neuroethics*, 1465-1471.

Racine, E., Waldman, S., Rosenberg, J., & Illes, J. (2010). Contemporary neuroscience in the media. *Social Science & Medicine, 71*, 725-733.

Racine, S. E., Keel, P. K., Burt, S. A., Sisk, C. L., Neale, M., Boker, S., & Klump, K. L. (2013). Exploring the relationship between negative urgency and dysregulated eating: Etiologic associations and the role of negative affect. *Journal of Abnormal Psychology, 122*(2), 433-444.

Raese, J. (2015). The pernicious effect of mind/body dualism in psychiatry. *Journal of Psychiatry, 18*, 219-226.

Raison, C. L., & Miller, A. H. (2011). Is depression an inflammatory disorder? *Current Psychiatry Reports, 13*(6), 467-475.

Ray, D. C., Armstrong, S. A., Balkin, R. S., & Jayne, K. M. (2015). Child-centered play therapy in the schools: Review and meta-analysis. *Psychology in the Schools, 52*(2), 107-123,

Ray, D. C., Bratton, S., Rhine, T., & Jones, L. (2001). The effectiveness of play therapy: Responding to the critics. *International Journal of Play Therapy, 10*(1), 85-108.

Read, J., Cartwright, C., Gibson, K., Shiels, C., & Haslam, N. (2014). Beliefs of people taking antidepressants about causes of depression and reasons for increased prescribing rates. *Journal of Affective Disorders, 168*, 236-242.

Read, J., Cartwright, C., Gibson, K., Shiels, C., & Magliano, L. (2015). Beliefs of people taking antidepressants about the causes of their own depression. *Journal of Affective Disorders, 174*, 150-156.

Read, J., Fosse, R., Moskowitz, A., & Perry, B. (2014). The traumagenic neurodevelopmental model of psychosis revisited. *Neuropsychiatry, 4*(1), 65-79.

Rabkin, J. G., Markowitz, J. S., Stewart, J., McGrath, P., Harrison, W., Quitkin, F. M., & Klein, D. F. (1986). How blind is blind? Assessment of patient and doctor medication guesses in a placebo-controlled trial of imipramine and phenelzine. *Psychiatry research, 19*(1), 75-86.

Read, J., Perry, B. D., Moskowitz, A., & Connolly, J. (2001). The contribution of early traumatic events to schizophrenia in some patients: A traumagenic neurodevelopmental model. *Psychiatry, 64*, 319-345.

Reiner, P. B. (2011). The rise of neuroessentialism. In J. Illes & B. J. Sahakian (Eds.), *Oxford handbook of neuroethics* (pp. 161-176). New York, NY: Oxford University Press.

Rigoni, D., & Brass, M. (2014). From intentions to neurons: Social and neural consequences of disbelieving in free will. *Topoi, 33*(1), 5-12.

Rigoni, D., Kühn, S., Gaudino, G., Sartori, G., & Brass, M. (2012). Reducing self-control by weakening belief in free will. *Consciousness and Cognition, 21*, 1482-1490.

Rigoni, D., Wilquin, H., Brass, M., & Burle, B. (2013). When errors do not matter: Weakening belief in intentional control impairs cognitive reaction to errors. *Cognition, 127*, 264-269.

Ripke, S., Wray, N. R., Lewis, C. M., Hamilton, S. P., Weissman, M. M., Breen, G., … & Degenhardt, F. (2013). A mega-analysis of genome-wide association studies for major depressive disorder. *Molecular Psychiatry, 18*(4), 497-511.

Robie, T. R. (1958). Iproniazid chemotherapy in melancholia. *The American Journal of Psychiatry, 115*, 402-409.

Roffman, J. L., Gerber, A. J., & Glink, D. M. (2012). Neural models of psychodynamic concepts and treatments: Implications for psychodynamic psychotherapy. In R. A. Levy, J. S. Ablon, & H. Kächele (Eds.), *Psychodynamic psychotherapy research: Evidence-based practice and practice-based evidence* (pp. 193-218). Totowa, NJ: Humana Press. http://dx.doi.org/10.1007/978-1-60761-792-1_11

Rogers, C. R. (1967). Some thoughts regarding the current presuppositions of the behavioral sciences. *Pastoral Psychology, 18*(8), 39-50.

Rogers, D., & Pies, R. (2008). General medical drugs associated with depression. *Psychiatry, 5*(12), 28-41.

Rose, S. L. (2013). Patient advocacy organizations: institutional conflicts of interest, trust, and trustworthiness. *The Journal of Law, Medicine & Ethics, 41*(3), 680-687.

Ross, C. A. (2013). Biology and genetics in DSM-5. *Ethical Human Psychology and Psychiatry, 15*, 195-198.

Rowlands, M. (2010). *The new science of the mind: From extended mind to embodied phenomenology*. Cambridge, MA: MIT Press.

Ruhé, H. G., Mason, N. S., & Schene, A. H. (2007). Mood is indirectly related to serotonin, norepinephrine and dopamine levels in humans: A meta-analysis of monoamine depletion studies. *Molecular Psychiatry, 12*(4), 331-359.

Rusch, L. C., Kanter, J. W., & Brondino, M. J. (2009). A comparison of contextual and biomedical models of stigma reduction for depression with a nonclinical undergraduate sample. *The Journal of nervous and mental disease, 197*(2), 104-110.

Rutherford, B. R., Wager, T. D., & Roose, S. P. (2010). Expectancy and the treatment of depression: A review of experimental methodology and effects on patient outcome. *Current Psychiatry Reviews, 6*(1), 1.

Rutherford, B. R., Wall, M. M., Brown, P. J., Choo, T. H., Wager, T. D., Peterson, B. S., ... & Roose, S. P. (2016). Patient expectancy as a mediator of placebo effects in antidepressant clinical trials. *American Journal of Psychiatry*, OnlineFirst, appi-ajp.

Ryan, V. & Edge, A. (2012). The role of play themes in non-directive play therapy. *Clinical Child Psychology and Psychiatry, 17*(3), 354-369.

Ryback, D. (2006). Self-determination and the neurology of mindfulness. *Journal of Humanistic Psychology, 46*, 474-493.

Sands, R. G. (1996). The elusiveness of identity in social work practice with women: A postmodern feminist perspective. *Clinical Social Work Journal, 24*(2), 167-186.

Sarama, J. & Clements, D. (2009). *Early childhood mathematics education research: Learning trajectories for young children*. New York, NY: Routledge.

Satel, S., & Lilienfeld, S. O. (2013). *Brainwashed: The seductive appeal of mindless neuroscience*. New York, NY: Basic Books.

Schaefer, C. E. & Drewes, A. (Eds.). (2013). *The therapeutic powers of play: Core agents of change*. New York, NY: John Wiley & Sons.

Schildkraut, J. J. (1965). The catecholamine theory of affective disorders: A review of supporting evidence. *American Journal of Psychiatry, 122*, 509-522.

Schmidt, U., Brown, A., McClelland, J., Glennon, D., & Mountford, V. A. (2016). Will a comprehensive, person-centered, team-based early intervention approach to first episode illness improve outcomes in eating disorders?. *The International Journal of Eating Disorders, 49*(4), 374-377.

Schomerus, G., Matschinger, H., & Angermeyer, M. C. (2014). Causal beliefs of the public and social acceptance of persons with mental illness: A comparative analysis of schizophrenia, depression and alcohol dependence. *Psychological Medicine, 44*(2), 303-314.

Schreiber, R., & Hartrick, G. (2002). Keeping it together: How women use the biomedical explanatory model to manage the stigma of depression. *Issues in Mental Health Nursing, 23*(2), 91-105.

Schroder, H. S., Dawood, S., Yalch, M. M., Donnellan, M. B., & Moser, J. S. (2016). Evaluating the Domain Specificity of Mental Health–Related Mind-Sets. *Social Psychological and Personality Science, 1948550616644657*, 1-13.

Schroder, H. S., Dawood, S., Yalch, M. M., Donnellan, M. B., & Moser, J. S. (2014). The role of implicit theories in mental health symptoms, emotion regulation, and hypothetical treatment choices in college students. *Cognitive Therapy and Research, 39*(2), 120-139.

Schultz, W. (2015)a. The chemical imbalance hypothesis: An evaluation of the evidence. *Ethical Human Psychology and Psychiatry, 17*(1), 60-75.

Schultz, W. (2015, August). Binge eating and genetics. Retrieved from https://www.madinamerica.com/2015/08/binge-eating-and-genetics/.

Schultz, W. (2015)b. Neuroessentialism: Theoretical and clinical considerations. *Journal of Humanistic Psychology*. doi:10.1177/0022167815617296

Schultz, W. (2016). Child-centered play therapy. *Reason Papers, 38*(1), 21-37.

Schultz, W., & Hunter, N. (2016)a. White paper: Brain scan research. *Ethical Human Psychology and Psychiatry, 18*(1), 9-19.

Schultz, W., & Hunter, N. (2016). Depression, chemical imbalances, and feminism. *Journal of Feminist Family Therapy, 28*(4), 159-173.

Schultz, W. (2017). Explaining depression in clinical settings: Shortcomings and dangers of simplified analogies. *Ethical Human Psychology and Psychiatry, 19*(1), 51-64.

Schultz, W. (2018). Biogenetic etiologies of mental disorders: Stigma, mental health literacy, and prognostic pessimism. *The Behavior Therapist, 41*(4), 188-194.

Schwartz, B., Bailey-Davis, L., Bandeen-Roche, K., Pollak, J., Hirsch, A. G., Nau, C., . . . Glass, T. A. (2014). Attention deficit disorder stimulant use, and childhood body mass index trajectory. *Pediatrics, 133*(4), 668-676.

Schwartz, T. L., & Petersen, T. (Eds.). (2016). *Depression: Treatment strategies and management.* New York, NY: Taylor and Francis.

Shin, J., Roughead, E. E., Park, B., & Pratt, N. L. (2016). Cardiovascular safety of methylphenidate among children and young people with attention-deficit/hyperactivity disorder (ADHD): Nationwide self-controlled case series study. *British Medical Journal, 353,* retrieved from http://www.bmj.com/content/353/bmj.i2550

Smart, J. J. C. (2008). The identity theory of mind. *Stanford Encyclopedia of Philosophy.* Retrieved from http://plato.stanford.edu/archives/fall2013/entries/mind-identity/

Shanmugasegaram, S., Russell, K. L., Kovacs, A. H., Stewart, D. E., & Grace, S. L. (2012). Gender and sex differences in prevalence of major depression in coronary artery disease patients: A meta-analysis. *Maturitas, 73,* 305-311.

Shore, P. A., Silver, S. L., & Brodie, B. B. (1955). Interaction of reserpine, serotonin, and lysergic acid diethylamide in brain. *Science, 122*(3163), 284-285.

Slaby, J., & Gallagher, S. (2014). Critical neuroscience and socially extended minds. *Theory, Culture & Society, 32*(1), 33-59.

Sloman, L., Price, J., Gilbert, P., & Gardner, R. (1994). Adaptive function of depression: psychotherapeutic implications. *American Journal of Psychotherapy, 48,* 401-416.

Smith, M. B. (1978). Humanism and behaviorism in psychology: Theory and practice. *Journal of Humanistic Psychology, 18,* 27-36.

Smith. P. K. (1997). Play fighting and real fighting. In A. Schmitt et al. (Eds.) *New Aspects of Human Ethology* (pp. 47-64). New York, NY: Plenum Press.

Sneed, J. R., Rutherford, B. R., Rindskopf, D., Lane, D. T., Sackeim, H. A., & Roose, S. P. (2008). Design makes a difference: A meta-analysis of antidepressant response rates in placebo-controlled versus comparator trials in late-life depression. *The American Journal of Geriatric Psychiatry, 16*(1), 65-73.

Sohn, M., Moga, D. C., Blumenschein, K., & Talbert, J. (2016). National trends in off-label use of atypical antipsychotics in children and adolescents in the United States. *Medicine, 95*(23). Retrieved from http://www.ncbi.nlm. nih.gov/pmc/articles/PMC4907659/

Spielmans, G. (2015). When marketing met science: Evidence regarding modern antidepressants and antipsychotic medications. *The Behavior Therapist, 38*(7), 199-205.

Spielmans, G. I., & Kirsch, I. (2014). Drug approval and drug effectiveness. *Annual Review of Clinical Psychology, 10*, 741-766.

Speerforck, S., Schomerus, G., Pruess, S., & Angermeyer, M. C. (2014). Different biogenetic causal explanations and attitudes towards persons with major depression, schizophrenia and alcohol dependence: Is the concept of a chemical imbalance beneficial? *Journal of Affective Disorders, 168*, 224-228.

Stagnitti, K. (2004). Understanding play: The implications for play assessment. *Australian Occupational Therapy Journal, 51*(1), 3-12.

Stark, E., & Flitcraft, A. H. (1988). Women and children at risk: A feminist perspective on child abuse. *International Journal of Health Services, 18*, 97-118.

Steen, M. (1991). Historical perspectives on women and mental illness and prevention of depression in women, using a feminist framework. *Issues in Mental Health Nursing, 12*(4), 359-374.

Stoppard, J. M. (1999). Why new perspectives are needed for understanding depression in women. *Canadian Psychology, 40*(2), 79-90.

Straker, M. (1959). Imipramine (tofranil): A safe, effective antidepressant drug in private practice. *Canadian Medical Association Journal, 80*(7), 546-549.

Szasz, T. S. (1974). *The myth of mental illness: Foundations of a theory of personal conduct.* New York, NY: Harper Perennial.

Szeszko, P. R., Robinson, D. G., Ikuta, T., Peters, B. D., Gallego, J. A., Kane, J., & Malhotra, A. K. (2014). White matter changes associated with antipsychotic treatment in first-episode psychosis. *Neuropsychopharmacology, 39*, 1324-1331.

Tambling, R. B. (2012). A literature review of therapeutic expectancy effects. *Contemporary Family Therapy, 34*(3), 402-415.

Teasdale, J. D., Segal, Z., & Williams, J. M. G. (1995). How does cognitive therapy prevent depressive relapse and why should attentional control (mindfulness) training help?. *Behaviour Research and Therapy, 33*(1), 25-39.

ten Brinke, L. F., Bolandzadeh, N., Nagamatsu, L. S., Hsu, C. L., Davis, J. C., Miran-Khan, K., & Liu-Ambrose, T. (2015). Aerobic exercise increases hippocampal volume in older women with probable mild cognitive impairment: A 6-month randomised controlled trial. *British Journal of Sports Medicine, 49*(4), 248–254. http://dx.doi.org/10.1136/bjsports-2013-093184

Turner, E. H., Matthews, A. M., Linardatos, E., Tell, R. A., & Rosenthal, R. (2008). Selective publication of antidepressant trials and its influence on apparent efficacy. *New England Journal of Medicine, 358*(3), 252-260.

Turns, B. A. & Kimmes, J. (2014). "I'm not the problem!" Externalizing children's 'problems' using play therapy and developmental considerations. *Contemporary Family Therapy, 26*(1), 135-147.

Udenfriend, S., Weissbach, H., & Bogdanski, D. F. (1957). Effect of iproniazid on serotonin metabolism in vivo. *Journal of Pharmacology and Experimental Therapeutics, 120*(2), 255-260.

Ussher, J. M. (2010). Are we medicalizing women's misery? A critical review of women's higher rates of reported depression. *Feminism & Psychology, 20*, 9-35.

Valenstein, E. (2002). *Blaming the brain: The truth about drugs and mental health.* New York, NY: Simon and Schuster.

Valenstein, E. S. (1998). *Blaming the brain: The truth about drugs and mental health.* New York, NY: Simon & Schuster.

van der Kolk, B. A. (2003). The neurobiology of childhood trauma and abuse. *Child and Adolescent Psychiatric Clinics of North America, 12*, 293-317.

Van Oudenhove, L., & Cuypers, S. (2014). The relevance of the philosophical "mind–body problem" for the status of psychosomatic medicine: A conceptual analysis of the biopsychosocial model. *Medicine, Health Care and Philosophy, 17*, 201-213.

Venkatasubramanian, G., & Keshavan, M. S. (2016). Biomarkers in psychiatry: a critique. *Annals of Neurosciences, 23*(1), 3-5.

Vintiadis, E. (2014). A frame of mind from psychiatry. *Medicine, Health Care and Philosophy, 18,* 523-532.

Vîslă, A., Constantino, M. J., Newkirk, K., Ogrodniczuk, J. S., & Söchting, I. (2016). The relation between outcome expectation, therapeutic alliance, and outcome among depressed patients in group cognitive-behavioral therapy. *Psychotherapy Research,* onlinefirst, 10.1080/10503307.2016.1218089, 1-11.

Visser, S. N., Danielson, M. L., Wolraich, M. L., Fox, M. H., Grosse, S. D., Valle, L. A., . . . Peacock, G. (2016). Vital signs: National and state-specific patterns of attention deficit/hyperactivity disorder treatment among insured children aged 2-5 years—United States, 2008-2014. *Morbidity and Mortality Weekly Report, 65,* 443-450.

Vohs, K. D., & Schooler, J. W. (2008). The value of believing in free will encouraging a belief in determinism increases cheating. *Psychological Science, 19*(1), 49-54.

Wakefield, J. C. (2014). Wittgenstein's nightmare: Why the RDoC grid needs a conceptual dimension. *World Psychiatry, 13*(1), 38-40.

Walter, H. (2013). The third wave of biological psychiatry. *Frontiers in Psychology, 4*(582), 1-8.

Wampold, B. E. & Imel, Z. E. (2015). *The great psychotherapy debate: The evidence for what makes psychotherapy work.* New York, NY: Routledge.

Watkins, E., & Teasdale, J. D. (2004). Adaptive and maladaptive self-focus in depression. *Journal of Affective Disorders, 82*(1), 1-8.

Wedge, M. (2016). *A disease called childhood: Why ADHD became an American epidemic.* New York, NY: Avery.

Weissman, M. M., Bland, R. C., & Canino, C. J. (1996). Cross national epidemiology of major depression and bipolar disorder. *Journal of the American Medical Association, 276,* 293-329.

Weisz, J. R., McCarty, C. A., & Valeri, S. M. (2006). Effects of psychotherapy for depression in children and adolescents: A meta-analysis. *Psychological Bulletin, 132*(1), 132-149.

Welzel, C. & Inglehart, R. (2010). Agency, values, and well-being: A human development model. *Social Indicators Research, 97*(1), 43-63.

Whitaker, R. (2010). *Anatomy of an epidemic: Magic bullets, psychiatric drugs, and the astonishing rise of mental illness in America.* New York, NY: Crown.

Whitaker, R., & Cosgrove, L. (2015). *Psychiatry under the influence: Institutional corruption, social injury, and prescriptions for reform.* New York, NY: Palgrave Macmillan.

Whitebread, D., Coltman, P., Jameson, H., & Lander, R. (2009). Play, cognition and self-regulation: What exactly are children learning when they learn through play? *Play and Learning in Educational Settings, 26*(2), 40-50.

Whooley, O. (2014). Nosological reflections, the failure of DSM-5, the emergence of RDoC, and the decontextualization of mental distress. *Society and Mental Health, 4*(2), 92-110.

Wiesjahn, M., Jung, E., Kremser, J. D., Rief, W., & Lincoln, T. M. (2016). The potential of continuum versus biogenetic beliefs in reducing stigmatization against persons with schizophrenia: An experimental study. *Journal of Behavior Therapy and Experimental Psychiatry, 50,* 231-237.

Wilson, M. (2002). Six views of embodied cognition. *Psychonomic Bulletin & Review, 9,* 625-636.

Winsor, T. (1954). Human pharmacology of reserpine. *Annals of the New York Academy of Sciences, 59*(1), 61-81.

Wolpert, L. (2008). Depression in an evolutionary context. *Philosophy, Ethics, and Humanities in Medicine, 3*(8), 1-3.

Wood, M. L. (1990). Naming the illness: the power of words. *Family Medicine, 23*(7), 534-538.

Wrosch, C., Scheier, M. F., Miller, G. E., Schulz, R. & Carver, C. S. (2003). Adaptive self-regulation of unattainable goals: Goal disengagement, goal reengagement, and subjective well-being. *Personality and Social Psychology Bulletin, 29*(12), 1494-1508.

Wunderink, L., Nieboer, R. M., Wiersma, D., Sytema, S., & Nienhuis, F. J. (2013). Recovery in remitted first-episode psychosis at 7 years of follow-up of an early dose reduction/discontinuation or maintenance treatment strategy: Long-term follow-up of a 2-year randomized clinical trial. *JAMA Psychiatry, 70*(9), 913-920.

Yanchar, S. C., & Hill, J. R. (2003). What is psychology about? Toward an explicit ontology. *Journal of Humanistic Psychology, 43,* 11-32.

Yeager, M. & Yeager, D. (2013). Self-regulation. In C. E. Schaefer & A. Drewes (Eds.), *The therapeutic powers of play: Core agents of change* (pp. 269-292). New York, NY: John Wiley & Sons.

Young, J. E., Klosko, J. S., & Weishaar, M. E. (2003). *Schema therapy: A practitioner's guide*. New York, NY: Guilford Press.

Zachar, P. (2000). *Psychological concepts and biological psychiatry: A philosophical analysis*. Philadelphia, PA: John Benjamins.

Zhao, X., Liu, L., Zhang, X. X., Shi, J. X., & Huang, Z. W. (2014). The effect of belief in free will on prejudice. *PLoS One, 9*(3), e91572.

Zimmerman, M., Ellison, W., Young, D., Chelminski, I., & Dalrymple, K. (2015). How many different ways do patients meet the diagnostic criteria for major depressive disorder?. *Comprehensive Psychiatry, 56*, 29-34.

 Index

Made in the USA
San Bernardino,
CA